MW00948762

Puppy Love

7 Secrets To Raising A Well Behaved Golden Retriever Puppy Who Listens And Loves You Back

Martina Annelie Becher

Puppy Love - 7 Secrets To Raising A Well Behaved Golden Retriever Puppy Who Listens And Loves You Back
Copyright © 2017 Martina Annelie Becher

ISBN-13: 978-1973701811
ISBN-10: 1973701812

Editing by John Freedom
Photographs by Klaus Leuscher, Verena Maier Rübsamen, Marc Jung and Martina Becher
Book design by Marc Jung and Sascha Zimmermann

In loving memory of my dearest Golden friends who taught me so much about our wonderful breed and left way too soon.

Patricia (Pat) Bush and Heather Morris — no words can express what you have done for our Goldens and what your friendship has meant to me.

Wheaton's Clemens (Sebastian) who brought the joy of Golden Retrievers back into my life.

Acknowledgements

What would the world's greatest author be without those who believe in him? How would he get his work finished without help and support?

Well, I am certainly not the world's greatest author but I have had fantastic support from some very special people!

First and foremost my sister Susanne who made this project possible in the first place. Having a sister like you, Susanne, is a great blessing!

My gratitude goes out to John Freedom who gently edited my book and helped me to express my thoughts well, even though I am not a native English speaker. John, thank you so much for doing all this for me and our wonderful breed!

Special thanks to Marc Jung who gave my book it's beautiful face. I don't know what I would have done without you, dear Marc!
And last but not least, thank you to all those wonderful Goldens who over almost fourty years have made my life happy and joyous – you are for ever in my heart and I am so blessed to have shared my time with you.

Thank you all so very much!

"*Golden Retrievers are a special breed, as are their owners. In this new book noted trainer and animal psychologist Martina Becher shows GR owners how to develop the kind of happy, respectful relationship they want with their dogs. Warm, witty and informative, it's filled with helpful tips, techniques and insights. This wonderful book deserves a wide readership both by GR owners, and by all who wish to understand and have a better relationship with man's best friend.*"

John Freedom, ACEP Research Coordinator and author, Heal Yourself with Emotional Freedom Technique

"*There are many books available today on 'Dog Training' and I find most are basically the same with slight variations on a similar message. Most have a few pages on young puppies, usually covering things like how big a box to buy and what sort of bowl is best etc. This book is different, it approaches, everything from the puppies viewpoint and it really does make you stop and think in a different way. I'm sure that many of the minor questions, queries and problems we have had over the years with new puppies and new puppy owners would not have occurred if the owners had read this book as part of their decision making process prior to having a new puppy as part of their family.*"

John Keene, breeder of Shinehill Golden Retrievers, United Kingdom

"*Very interesting, fact-based puppy (and dog) training and addicting as so easy to read. A must for every Golden Retriever puppy owner.*"

Christine Bugiel, Breeder of Dailuaine Golden Retrievers in Germany

Table of Contents

A personal Message From Martina:

Dear Golden Puppy Perosn, I am so happy that you have decided to learn the Secrets of Puppy Love by getting my book. You will find it a treasure to help you raise your puppy so she listens and loves you back .

In a nutshell, here is what you'll learn:

⤷ Reaching your goals

▶ *Become your Golden Retriever's favourite person, the one she will love with all her heart, the one she will look up to for guidance and who means the world to her.*

▶ *Understand your puppy's development and psychology and educate him to be the most wonderful friend you could ever wish for.*

▶ *Learn how to express your love for your puppy in a way that supports his development and helps him become a great personality.*

▶ *Become the perfect person for that unique puppy of yours and make your dream come true!*

▶ *Take the first steps to training your youngster without intimidation or force; learn how to quickly and safely train him to go toilet outside, to feel safe and secure in your home; teach him to stay on his own for a while when you need to go out.*

▶ *Learn how to train your Golden Retriever to get fast and proven results in harmony with his own nature.*

Enjoy!

Martina

This unique book will help you to create the most awesome relationship with your little Golden friend. By following the easy step-by-step plan I have outlined for you, you will be able to easily understand your puppy so that you can teach her all she needs to know and have fun doing it.

Being a dog parent has been your dream for a long time and now you have finally decided to make that dream come true. Congratulations because this is your first step into a wonderful new life full of beautiful and rewarding experience!

By choosing a Golden Retriever you have decided to share your life with a dog who will do his very best to never let you down. His beauty, gentleness, biddability and his great will to please are his greatest assets. Easy to train and always ready to forgive he will soon mature into the friend of a lifetime.

⮑ Your Golden's assets

But Golden Retrievers are very special!

Not only are they biddable and gentle, they also like to carry things, some of them do it all day long. They don't care what it is, as long as it can be picked up and carried!

This Golden habit will change your life for ever, I promise you. Your shoes and boots, your socks and jumpers, your scarf and even the remote TV control don't really belong to you any more. They now belong to your Retriever! Even though he may have toys you call "his", he has some very different ideas on the subject. Life is just not worth living if, as a Retriever, you ain't got nothing to carry!

Objects will be scattered all over and you will spend endless hours looking for something only to find it in his basket somewhere. The upside of this is that you will always be greeted with a present when you come home and so will your visitors; the downside is that you will have to become just that little bit more careful to put your most valuable possessions into a "Golden-proof place".

At the moment your future big boy or girl is still a little puppy with soft fur and big dark eyes. Being with her, enjoying precious moments is so much fun for both of you. Almost to the degree that you sometimes wish she would stay forever your little baby.

⊃ Questions you may be asking yourself sooner or later

At the same time having a puppy is quite an adventure. Many questions arise during the days and nights. Sometimes you and your family may feel overwhelmed and wonder if getting a puppy was indeed the right decision, or if it might have been better to get a somewhat older Golden Retriever.

On the other hand having a puppy is your unique chance to really make sure that your dog gets all the right treatment right from the start. That he is not being mistreated, neglected or trained the wrong way. You want him to trust people, to feel safe and secure and to develop into a great personality. You want his life to be happy from the word "go" and you are willing to do all it takes to create that loving, trusting friendship both of you deserve.

You know deep inside that in order to become the dog of your dreams your youngster needs you to be a *very patient and loving parent and teacher.* You have high expectations, you really want to be the best you can be when it comes to training and looking after your puppy.

➲ Being a patient and loving parent and teacher

It is my pleasure to assist you in this! To help you become that great dog parent your Golden Retriever deserves and to feel that unique connection with your dog. To get the great feeling of owning a dog who behaves well, no matter what the circumstance and knowing that this beautiful Golden Retriever is your special friend.

But I know that there is *so much* to learn before this state of mutual happiness can be experienced on a permanent and lasting basis.

⮑ Train and trust yourself

Over the years I have come to realize that *dog training is an inside job*, that you *need to train yourself* before you can train your dog and that you have to *trust yourself* before your Golden can trust you.

⮑ The Truth Based Golden Retriever Education System

Forty years of living with and caring for our wonderful breed have taught me that there are many ways you can go wrong, and there are many roads which will lead to a life full of pain and misery. From my life's experience as an owner, breeder, trainer and breed advisor and thanks to all the teachings I received from some of the most influential people in the breed, I developed **The Truth Based Golden Retriever Education System**. It is the backbone of the cutting-edge knowledge and secrets I am going to share with you here.

Unlike many other dog training modalities this system is completely free from any form of unfriendliness towards your puppy. You also don't have to become an Alpha Dog for your puppy to look up at you and be guided by you. You can be yourself because your dog loves you as you are!

⊃ No unfriendlyness
⊃ No Alpha Dog

The basis of the **The Truth Based Golden Retriever Education System** are scientifically proven facts about puppies and dogs, their developmental stages and a sound knowledge of the human psyche. *When you combine present day information about dogs with knowledge about your own behaviour and psyche you are armed with a road map that will guide you and your puppy safely to the place of love and mutual understanding.*

⊃ Instead: love and mutual under-standing

This book is such a road map. When you follow the steps I have outlined, you will reach your goal of becoming a great dog parent and a fantastic friend for your Golden Retriever. Bringing up your puppy will still be work but it will lose its stressfulness and worry.

A most exciting, wonderful time lies ahead of you: a time you will remember for the rest of your life. Watching your Golden Retriever grow, being part of

⊃ Exciting times lying ahead of you

the miracle will warm your heart. Having a puppy come and stay with you is a great pleasure because she brings so much fun, light heartedness and humour to your home. Friends and family will come just to see and adore her and to be enchanted by her magic.

⊃ *The* puppy becoming *your* puppy

But that's not all. There is going to be that very special moment when "the puppy" suddenly turns into "your puppy". The day when all of a sudden she recognizes you, not just as a kind human being and generous caretaker but as that very special, unique person she has given her heart to. From that moment on she will be happy to see you – not because you are someone but because you are you! And this will be the beginning of a life-long deep and lasting love relationship.

Getting a dog, buying a puppy is always a commitment. With it comes great responsibility. Bringing up a Golden Retriever puppy is very rewarding but it is also a lot of work. Being there for someone 24/7 really takes some doing, and you will have countless questions on how to do things right.

By answering your most pressing questions and by guiding you through the rough currents of looking after a bundle of life full of zest and mischief this book will enable to raise your puppy effortlessly and have fun doing it.

Instead of worrying about the "How – To's" and "Whys" you'll have plenty of time to play with your baby. You will come to realize that it can be very easy to educate and guide your puppy, to teach him all he needs to know about life.

You know how first time puppy parents sometimes go to great length to get some good advice and how they try all sorts of things to get from A to B because they suddenly feel so overwhelmed by their puppy's behaviour?

Well, this won't be you!

By understanding your pups developmental needs and by learning how to communicate your wishes in a way that puppy can understand you will have that "magic blueprint" for a well trained, happy dog. You will be able to avoid those mistakes that make a dog's life a misery and the owner extremely unhappy. You will not need to ask every other dog owner in sight for advice nor experiment with different dog training modalities which lead to confusion and sometimes even hardship.

➲ Understanding your pup's needs avoids making mistakes

You will instead follow your heart and your own inner wisdom and let your love guide your way.

Puppy times soon pass. Your baby will soon be a beautiful youngster and then a great Golden Retriever. The more you can enjoy the springtime of your friend's life the more rewarding the summer and autumn will be.

And when the inevitable winter will arrive after 10 or 14 years you will be able to look back onto a lifetime full of happy times you spent with your Golden friend.

The baby steps are the most important steps any young being takes, and it is your great pleasure to walk those steps with your Golden puppy now. By gently helping him to learn about life, to develop his personality and to cope with life's challenges you yourself will grow and learn a lot. Dogs are great teachers and your Golden Retriever has come to you for a reason.

⮑ The most important steps in life

This reason includes making you happy beyond measure and to assure you that you have a faithful friend right by your side.

No matter what your plans are, whether you just want to be a Retriever parent, an exhibitor or someone who takes part in working events – *the first year is the foundation of it all.*

By choosing to follow the **Truth Based Golden Retriever Education System** you will learn to bring up your puppy on the basis of sound principles and strategies which will make the process easy and effortlessly.

Creating your own solutions and finding your own answers will be no longer a problem but an enjoyable process.

As you already know, Happiness is a Golden Retriever puppy – or, as many Golden parents put it: Happiness is Golden! And the roads two faithful friends travel together begin with the first steps. So let's make your puppy's first steps with you happy and cheerful!

Fast and proven results

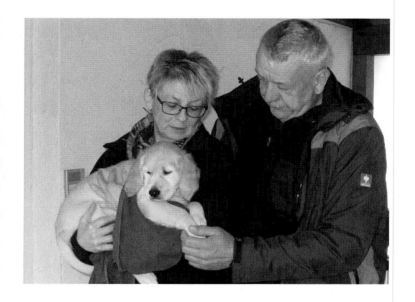

We will always love you

Here are the long term results I am getting on a regular basis with all of the puppies I bring up and educate with the **Truth Based Golden Retriever Education System:**

⮌ An easy to manage, very obedient Golden...

All my Goldens are *easy to manage* and *very obedient* no matter where we go or whom we meet. *They are able be on their own,* inside the house as well as in the car or in a hotel room. *Friendly* towards people they are my neighbours' favourites. They *come to the whistle* no matter what, and *always come* when called. I can walk them *on the lead* and *off the lead* even in the forest or when we meet aggressive canines. They *follow* the horse when I am out on horseback and enjoy going out with me when I am on my bicycle.

⮌ ... friendly,
⮌ ... coming to the whistle when called,

⮌ ... feeling safe,

They *feel safe* with family and friends in case I have to leave them somewhere.

⮌ ... eager to learn,

They are *eager to learn* anything I am eager to teach them, they *play a lot* and like to make friends with other dogs.

But most important of all, they *always look at me for guidance and feel that we are family and that I am the one who guides them into the right directions.*

➲ ...looking for guidance.

My Goldens *sit on the sofa* with me and come into bed in the morning to say "hello". They *get off* the sofa and bed when *I ask them* to and they allow me to take all their bones and toys away from them. They are *full of trust and patience,* even when we need to see the vet.

Our life together is relaxed and easy. I know that I can rely on my dogs and they know that they can rely on me.

Problems and Roadblocks

⊃ Pitfalls

But most people can't rely on their Goldens to that extent. They find it extremely difficult to get their friends to come back to them once they have been let off the lead. Walking them on the lead is more like a struggle than a pleasure for many Golden Retriever owners. Their dogs chew on table legs and scratch doors in order to be let out. Attending puppy classes and dog school for month after month does not seem to get them anywhere.

When their Goldens are small they feel that bringing up a puppy is hard work and difficult to do. In fact they are just waiting for time to pass so that the baby is not a baby anymore but an adult who is well behaved.

New puppy owners feel overwhelmed because they have very little knowledge about puppies and their needs. They can't seem to find the help they need to make things easy for themselves and their little ones.

Why is it that so many owners fail at bringing up their puppy for lifelong happiness?

The Roadblocks

Since all puppy parents set out with the intention to do their best in order to bring up their puppy there must be some pretty common roadblocks to happiness most of them stumble upon. Researching this I have encountered five categories of roadblocks:

Roadblock #1

➲ Roadblock #1: The Golden's reputation of being friendly, kind an easy to manage. - The perfect beginner's dog.

This first roadblock has to do with the reputation of the Golden Retriever as such and the personalities of those who feel attracted to the breed.

Over the years the Golden Retriever has gained a reputation as being friendly, kind and easy to manage – in short the perfect dog for inexperienced people who don't care much for dog training or obedience. Many of those who get a Golden Retriever puppy expect their dog to be good and well behaved from birth. They firmly believe that a Golden Retriever needs no proper education because of his genes.

Adding to this comes the fact that due to his reputation and beauty the breed attracts people who are kind and loving themselves, who love to make others happy, even to the degree of putting their own interests behind other's wants and needs.

The downside of this kindness is a strong tendency to say "Yes" rather than "No" even when a "No" is warranted and finding it difficult to set and reinforce boundaries. Many Golden Retriever owners believe that saying "No" hurts others and that is something they don't want to do. Due to all this they are very reluctant to set firm boundaries for their beloved dogs and tend not to restrict them, often to the degree of letting them get on with whatever it is.

This training reluctance leads to the fact that many poor Goldens are denied good education and as a result have to endure Haltis, choke chains, being shut away in crates, or denied the freedom of a good run around. This is not because their owners are bad people – it is the price both dogs and owners have to pay for the owners just not teaching their dog good manners. An untrained Golden Retriever is no pleasure to be with because he needs a good education and firm boundaries just like any other dog.

Roadblock #2

The second one is that very often people who get a Golden don't seem to be clear on the kind of life they want to lead with their dog. They have no goals and no plan on how to get to a place of happiness. They assume that things will just work out right somehow which they hardly ever do.

Roadblock #3

The third roadblock is *"Dog Owner Naiveté"*. This is when perfectly clever and capable people place their dog's fate in the hands of so-called experts. Even when they feel and know what would be best for their Goldens and themselves they still follow advice and guidance which is contrary to their own knowledge and experience. They feel incompetent but that is not the real problem. Most people are very competent when it comes to bringing up a puppy – it's just that they don't believe in themselves and rather follow the advice of others than following their own hearts.

Roadblock #4

Often puppy parents don't really have the time they need to invest in the upbringing and education of their young Golden. So they struggle along, leaving their pups with family members or on their own very soon after getting them and hope that all will work out well somehow.

⊃ Roadblock #4: Lacking time

Roadblock #5

Last but not least is the lack of present day knowledge about domestic dogs, their development and needs. This includes a lack of understanding about dogs' brains and nervous systems.

⊃ Roadblock #5: Lacking knowledge about development and needs

Amongst other things these roadblocks express themselves in *impatience* and the *wrong training ideas*.

▶ The lack of time leads to the feeling that the puppy is taking too long over being house trained, is taking too long over learning how to be alone and is taking to long over being obedient. *So the owners feel under pressure to speed up the process and get stressed out when puppy needs more time than they planned for.*

▶ Because they don't have a clear picture in their minds of where they want to get to with their puppy and no realistic time frame to reach their goals they feel dissatisfied with the way things are going. *The puppy notices that something is wrong somewhere and reacts in its own way to the stressful situation.*

▶ Living in a clean, orderly house is a top priority for many people. They feel that their possessions define the quality of their lives so there is little room for fun and play and the untidiness a puppy causes. *Again, the puppy is experienced as someone who causes stress.*

With so many unpleasant feelings connected to the developmental process each puppy goes through in her own time frame, puppy parents often find it extremely difficult to relax and enjoy their pups first month in their homes. They don't realize how important fun and play are for the creation of a lifelong relationship based on love and trust.

Because they can't take the time to slowly and thoroughly educate their pups according to their developmental stages, owners either *work too hard* at it when the puppy is **too young** to understand or they *leave it too late* which again makes things more difficult to teach and learn.

Most owners do not realize *that they need to train themselves first before they can train a dog.* Depending on their personalities they are either too lenient or too strict.

But **each** and **every one** of those roadblocks can be overcome. They are not set in stone as the following story reveals.

⮑ Overcoming those roadblocks

Find out how Maggy's owners managed to create the perfect relationship despite of all the roadblocks.

Maggy's Story

Lisa and John were very experienced Golden Retriever owners who had sadly lost their latest golden girl due to cancer at the age of seven. Being in their early sixties they felt too old to have another puppy but finally could not live without a Golden Retriever. So little Maggy came to make them happy again.

After the first few days, in which all was sweet and wonderful, Lisa began to feel that bringing up a pup was hard work. Whenever we spoke on the phone I could sense her impatience and frustration because little Maggy was either doing "this" wrong or not doing "that" right. They had started taking her to a puppy class right from the word "go" where she picked up a tummy bug and learned some unruly behaviour. Due to all the excitement and distraction created by all the other puppies in the class Maggy couldn't really concentrate on her lessons and learned to pull on the lead and "How not to come when called".

By expecting too much from her too early the couple got quite emotional over little Maggy's ways. She would play "catch me if you can" with them when out in the garden and had started to please herself when out on walks.

At that point Lisa asked me for help with Maggy's training because she didn't want her girl to get into the habit of chasing after wildlife in the woods.

Going for a walk with them I quickly detected the "**5 I's**" – *impatience, inconsistency, insensitivity, irrationality* and even *insecurity* in action.

So we started all over from scratch. Lisa and her husband really needed to educate themselves to be more consistent, less impatient and *less* tolerant when it came to training their youngster. At the same time they needed to understand the importance of respecting the *brain development stages* and *neuronal pathway creation process* in their pup's central nervous system.

Realizing all this and changing their own behavioural patterns wasn't easy for them because over the years they had picked up some of the most powerful dog training myths. Those myths had shaped the way they saw and interpreted their dog's behaviour and had also led them to react to Maggy in certain ways. Adding to that came the fact that they had a personal tendency to just watch things happen and so they just didn't move fast enough to stop Maggy from doing what she was doing. They would just stand

and watch her pick up some dirt in the fields without taking it out of her fang or even chasing her off. By not interrupting her undesirable behaviour by either being too slow or by not watching her closely enough they actually *supported* the development of neural pathways in Maggy's brain which then expressed as unwanted behavioural patterns.

On the other hand they did not take advantage of her inborn need to follow by playing hide and seek in safe places which could have taught her to stay with them right from a very early age.

Lisa and John were really committed to learning how to teach their puppy how to behave well. They studied the principles of the **Truth Based Golden Retriever Education System** and decided to re-train themselves so they could then train little Maggy.

They did this by watching their own actions, supporting each other by pointing out unproductive or wrong behavioural patterns and training themselves to be less tolerant with unruly behaviours but also more rewarding when Maggy did the right things. They did all they could to react more consistently and to communicate their intentions more clearly and learned to read Maggy's intentions before she acted them out. Over the period of a few month Lisa and John managed to change their expectations as well as their perceptions. Looking at their own and little Maggy's behaviour patterns in a completely new way gave them the opportunity to create more happiness for all of them.

Today little Maggy comes when called, walks on the lead without pulling and is very happy to be with her human family. And, needless to say, the family is very, very happy to have her.

⮑ My mistakes.

My Own Story

I should have known better!

I had once been in Lisa's place too. After having owned three wonderful female Goldens who were ever so sweet and easy to educate I got my first male. He was a very happy, boisterous chap. Of course I took him out to play with another Golden of the same age and also to training classes right away. In those days I believed, as many still do today, that puppies are best trained in a puppy class. I also believed that puppies need to play for hours without human interruption. This led my youngster to believe that life was all about running around and pleasing yourself.

Over time he developed into a very big, strong specimen who thought life was wonderful. His temperament was sweet, there was not a growl in him but he saw no reason to do as he was told when he didn't want to. He was impossible on the lead and quite a few times almost tore my arm out when he suddenly charged forwards because he had seen something. No matter what I tried to make things better it just did not work.

My then husband and I could not agree on any training regimen. Even though I was working as a dog trainer at that time and my students became very successful through my teachings my ex husband saw no use in those principles I taught. He was very inconsistent by giving commands to the dog but never following through. This led to utter confusion in the poor dog since I was doing my best to reinforce my commands whilst my husband did the opposite.

↪ Inconsistent commands resulting in confusion.

Adding to this came the fact that due to a heavy workload, financial struggles and a very frustrating relationship both of us were sad and bad tempered at times.

↪ Personal problems increasing confusion.

All this confusion hurt the development of our much loved dog. Of course he got showered with our feelings and energies because dogs DO pick up on the emotions of their humans in a very sensitive way. Today we know that dogs share our emotions, that they read our minds and know exactly what goes on inside of us. This means that *our dogs suffer when we suffer and they're happy when we are happy.*

But what is scientifically proven by now was not known all those years ago simply because we did not have the technology.

⮕ Helpless-
ness resulting
in injustice.

I got very upset and unjust with my poor dog, and, sad to say, my emotions got the better of me quite a few times. I loved him dearly but felt quite helpless at the same time. Love and helplessness are not a good mixture when it comes to dog training.

In those days no one thought about the brain. The human brain was still a mystery yet to be discovered and so it was no wonder that the dog's brain and nervous system were never considered important factors in the development of a canine. When it came to puppies growing into dogs, brain development didn't exist.

Falling into the dominance trap

Instead of reflecting on brain and central nervous system development people saw unwanted dog behaviour in the light of *the dominance theory*. This theory, which is one of the great myths in the dog – world explains unruly behaviour by assuming that the unruly dog is out to dominate his human companions. Because of that the human needs to be more dominant than the dog. This myth can greatly damage the trust between an owner and his dog.

⊃ Dominance theory.

Since the teachers of the dominance theory had such convincing arguments I forgot all about my psychological knowledge and began to believe that my dog was out to dominate me. Nothing could have been further from the truth but at the time I couldn't see it any other way. So in a way I tried to be more dominant myself. Not only did that strategy not work for either of us, it caused me to act against my inner conviction, making my Golden and myself quite unhappy. Looking back it was a hard and upsetting time.

⊃ "Convincing" arguments

Happy again at last!

⮡ Leaving
dominance
theory behind.

I finally decided I'd stop worrying about dominance and drop the idea of having to show my Golden who's the boss. Since the dominance theory had become such a powerful tool in the dog training world I decided to opt out for some time and give up my dog trainer's ambitions. So I just leaned back and enjoyed the last years I could spend together with my dog.

Then, after all that frustration and pain I waited for almost two years before getting another Golden Retriever to share my life. It was a long and lonely time!

When my new puppy Sebastian arrived I listened to my heart and let him guide me along the way.

This meant giving him all the time he needed to develop his character and body, patiently adjusting his lessons to his growing brain and abilities. Right from the beginning I helped him not to learn unwanted behavioural patterns such as pulling on the lead or playing "catch me if you can". I established just four rules and made sure we both stuck to them no matter what. Because I was single there was no one there to counteract my training.

Here are those 4 rules:

1. **always** come when called

2. **never** pull on the lead

3. **always** stand still and not move again at the word "wait"

4. **immediately** stop doing whatever it is at the words "No" and "Stop It"

⊃ Establishing 4 simple rules.

By me following his development and avoiding myth-based training he was able to grow into one of the happiest dogs I have ever met in my entire life. His trust in people and in himself was unshakeable, he loved everyone and everyone loved him. Sebastian really taught me the secret of bringing up puppies for lifelong happiness.

Sunshine, my other dog was brought up the same way and with the same effect. Now I am living with him and Sweetheart, a girl who is at the time of writing 16 weeks old and such a joy to have.

⊃ Learning from Sebastian

The Myths Of The Dog Training Industry

This is how it all begins

Many people can't learn from their Goldens because they still believe in the countless myths of the dog training industry.

⮑ 7 myths

These myths influence our point of view and our behaviour towards our puppies in unhelpful ways. Unless we recognize them as myths and not a truths we treat our dogs in a way which may be in opposition to our intentions. We may, *indeed cause the harm we wish to avoid.*

Myth #1 The Dominance Myth or Alpha Dog Myth

⮑ The Dominance Myth or Alpha Dog Myth.

The Dominance Myth explains the relationship between you and your Golden Retriever on the basis of a pecking order. It stems from the idea that dog societies work under a very strict hierarchy of Top Dog versus Low Dog, just as wolf packs are said to do.

The basis for this myth is the assumption, that our present day Golden Retrievers are run by the exact instincts and behaviour traits as were their ancestors, the wolves.

The Dominance Myth makes life complicated because it has several rules attached to it which, if violated, are said to pave the road to trouble:

Myth Rule 1

A Golden Retriever must not sleep in your bedroom because this would make him feel superior to you.

Myth Rule 2

Your dog must never be allowed into your bed or on the sofa, nor lay in the doorway because that would give him the feeling of being boss.

Myth Rule 3

You always need to feed yourself before you feed your dog because that's how it is in nature.
In a nutshell this Myth is all about being an Alpha Dog in your own home.

Can the Dominance Theory really be right? I don't think so!

Here are my questions:

1. Who has ever lived as a member of a pack of wolves at the time when dogs and wolf split up and knows for sure how they did behave all those millennia ago?

2. Is the behaviour wolves show in captivity today the same as their behaviour all those thousands of years ago? Who is out there in the wild now watching and documenting true wolf behaviour? And do wolves in captivity behave the same way as those who run free?

3. Under the assumption that there is something called co-evolution, i.e. two species evolving together and in relation to each other – what are the chances that man and dog did not?

I mean, how great is the possibility that Golden Retrievers have not fine tuned their behavioural patterns and instincts to living within the human family? Especially since they were bred to be biddable companions and co-workers?

If you believe in the Dominance Myth your life will become very difficult because you will have to follow all those rules to keep your puppy in his place in the pecking order of your home. You will have to make sure you always go through doors first, you never cuddle or give attention to him when he comes up asking for some and so on and so forth.

And all this hassle will *not improve* the relationship you have with your puppy. The effect of the Dominance Myth is that you feel threatened by your pup on a subconscious level and always need to be on guard. This Myth damages the trust between you and your Golden.

By believing in this myth you will actually destroy your and his happiness rather than create it.

Myth #2 All dogs are the same so the training must be the same for all dogs

⊃ All dogs are the same so the training must be the same for all dogs.

This can't be right either because breeders have gone to great length to create highly specialized breeds for different tasks.

In order to fulfil certain job descriptions dogs needed to have different personalities and character traits. Imagine a sheepdog in the hills in Turkey being as placid as a Golden Retriever! The wolves would soon have him for supper as well as eating the sheep he is supposed to protect.

Or think of a modern day guard dog species like the Russian Terrier who is alert, fast and fearless enough to guard large properties — would you say that such a dog has the same temperament as a Golden whose job it was to retrieve wounded pheasants and ducks alive after the hunter had shot them?

Certainly not!

So when it comes to handling and training the Golden has his own requirements. He needs to be addressed in a way that meets his biddability and great will to please as well as his sensitivity. No dog should ever be rough handled, but from experience I can assure you that a Schnauzer or Terrier sometimes needs to be spoken to in a way which would make a typical Golden Retriever shrink. Our Goldens are softer than many other breeds and this needs to be taken into account at all times.

Myth #3 Puppies do unwanted things because they want to test their people

The assumption that a puppy does things to "test" who is boss is wrong. A puppy does not have the brain to test his human caretakers. He is learning how to behave in a strange and sometimes even alien world, does not yet understand the rules nor the language of those around him.

⮑ Puppies do unwanted things because they want to test their people.

If he does not do as he is told or tries to get away from things he is just doing the best he can with the knowledge and experience of his young life and brain.

This myth is a very *dangerous one* because it is likely to aggravates the owners on a conscious and subconscious level. Who without getting annoyed would swallow insubordination? If and when you assume that your puppy or youngster is just testing boundaries, seeing how far he can go you may tend to immediately and automatically switch to the "I'll teach you" response. This will lead you into more forceful, less loving behaviour and can, in the long run, cause your puppy to become afraid of you.

➲ The puppy knows when it has done something wrong.

Myth #4 The puppy knows when it has done something wrong

False again! Don't believe this myth many owners have fallen for. A puppy **can not** remember things the way we humans can.

If she has done something unwanted and makes herself small when you come into the room after the "deed" this is because she reads your body language and feels threatened by your anger. The moment you discover the mess your physiology changes, whether you are aware of it or not. Stress hormones change the chemical set up of your body and you start smelling differently. This is immediately picked up by your dog and hence her fearful look. It is **by no means** a sign of a bad conscience or a feeling of guilt.

Myth #5 Puppies need to be put on a lead or they will run away

⮑ Puppies need to be put on a lead or they will run away.

No, puppies have an inborn instinct to follow because being left behind spells death for any young creature. That's why you don't need to put a pup on a lead when you take her out to a safe place.

Myth #6 Puppies learn best in puppy classes

⮑ Puppies learn best in puppy classes.

Not really. A puppy class is fun for owners and puppies alike but due to all that's going on the puppies can't concentrate on their lessons. Depending on the set up puppies can even get traumatized in a class if there is to much rough housing going on or if older dogs are allowed to "teach" the younger ones how to behave.

➲ Your dog is your partner and as such able to decide for himself

Myth #7 Your dog is your partner and as such able to decide for himself

Another common misunderstanding is that your dog is your partner and can and should decide many things for himself. In this scenario you don't educate your dog as such but let him do what he wants to do most of the time. This is a very modern myth which is again a very dangerous one.

This is similar to 'permissive parenting' styles many parents are using now. In a canine society dogs would mature into responsible individuals who are able to reach decisions and follow through with them. But we live in a human society and so it is our responsibility to make sure that our dogs behave well and are kept safe. The dog can never be a partner as we traditionally define the term. Making your dog your partner would cause great suffering and pain in the long run.

There are people however who keep a dog as a replacement for human companionship. Doing this tries to convert the dog into being someone he is not. Disappointment is inevitable.

This list of myths is by no means complete. I just gave you some ideas about the most favoured ones you may come across but have not yet mentioned the **Greatest Myth** of all:

⊃ The greatest myth of all .

> This is that dog training is about training a dog and that it is the dog who is responsible for his behaviour to the point where he can freely choose which way he wants to behave. **The truth is**: Dog training is an *inside job*. As uncomfortable as this may seem, we need to train ourselves first before we can train a dog.

We need to trust ourselves before anyone else can trust us. Why should my dog trust me if I don't trust myself? Why should he do what I say if I myself don't do what I say? Why should he respect me if I don't respect myself? Wouldn't that be expecting something that *no one* could deliver?

⊃ Trusting yourself.

All those myths were created because people were looking for solutions to the questions which move to a greater or lesser degree all dog owners.

▶ Why does my dog do this? (Whatever "This" happens to be.)

▶ What can I do about it, i.e. how can I influence my dog's behaviour so that he does what I want him to do?

In the past the question of "what makes a dog tick"? could only be answered through assumptions and interpretations of their behaviour. People used what ever knowledge there was to attempt to solve the mystery of canine behaviour.

At the same time people were also wondering about human habit and behaviour. Slowly but surely the brain and nervous system came into focus and with the new technologies the miracle of human feelings and behaviour began to reveal itself.

It is very interesting to note that lots of insights into the functioning of the nervous system and the brain were actually derived from animal testing. Many of those unhappy subjects were and are dogs.

Brain physiology and the existence of neurotransmitters were first discovered through examination of how animal brains work and much of today's scientific knowledge in psychology stems from early experiments carried out on – Dogs.

Isn't it strange that even though the brain physiology and much of what we know of the psychology of dogs have been known for years no one ever thought of integrating that knowledge into dog parenting and dog training?

That those scientifically proven facts are still being ignored today whilst thousands and thousands of dogs still being are subjected to myth based training techniques?

You don't need to believe these myths any more because you are now learning a way of educating both yourself and your puppy for a life full of happiness and bliss *which firmly rests on scientifically proven facts.*

In the next chapters I will show you how you can support your pups' development and maturation process in a way that will guarantee you the results you hope for.

After all, now that you have finally made your dream come true and got yourself that very special Golden Retriever puppy you will want to make sure everything works out right between the pair of you.

⊃ Outlook

The secrets I have discovered after more than 40 years of experience with Goldens of all ages are supported by my scientific training as Psychologist.

The **Truth Based Golden Retriever Education System** is a fast, safe and proven way to reaching your goals with your puppy and to becoming the dog owner you've always wanted to be!

The Truth Based Golden Retriever Education System

My Golden Family Gloria, Sunshine and Sweetheart

⊃ The parts

This system, which rests firmly on scientifically proven facts about dogs and their development as well as present day knowledge about the human psyche is made up of four major parts. These are Truth Based:

▶ **Golden Retriever Parenting**
▶ **Puppy Education and Training**
▶ **Adult Education and Training**
▶ **Health Care**

Each of these will give you clear conceptional knowledge as well as easy to follow step-by-step strategies. Applying the principles and following the strategies will give you fast and proven results with a Golden Retriever of any age.

⊃ 3 essential steps

The Golden Retriever Education System follows three essential steps:

1. **Know what you want**
2. **Get clear and concise information**
3. **Put that knowledge and information into wise, loving and consistent action**

You can only reach your goal if you have one. You can only get to where you want to get if you know How To get there and you will only be successful if you take action.

⊃ Step 1: Know what you want.

This simple truth applies to all areas of life but strangely enough is often ignored when it comes to bringing up children, raising and educating dogs or maintaining relationships. Many people seem to think that success in those most important areas of human life comes by the way, that you can just wing it and be happy.

But reality teaches us differently. Marriages break up, children leave their parents in a state of unhappiness and behavioural problems in dogs are on the rise.

When disaster strikes people sadly ask: *"What did I do wrong?"* and *"What could I have done to avoid this problem before it became too big to handle?"*

The truth is that in everyday life we often follow our emotions rather than our reasoning, and by doing so we sometimes hurt and upset those closest to us.

We act on the spur of the moment without considering the outcome. This is true for personal relationships and it is also true when it comes to dealing with our dogs.

Since our dogs depend on us we need to realize that whatever we do with them or to them makes them either happy or unhappy. This great responsibility is the reason why we must be very clear on what we expect from our Goldens, how we want them to behave and be. Our dog's happiness depends on our love for them and on the degree to which we are happy with their behaviours. If we fail to teach our dogs good manners we will, in the long run, become frustrated and likely to resent them.

The outcome may be that the dog develops really difficult behaviour, becomes aggressive or anxious. By not knowing how you want your dog to behave and how you would like him to be in himself, you prevent lifelong happiness for him and may, in the end, even have to re-home him.

Once you know how you would like your dog to behave, the things you want him to know and do as well as the behaviours you don't want you can teach him to fulfill your wishes. If you don't know what makes you happy, how is your dog supposed to know?

But knowing what you want is not enough – you need the knowledge to back up your ideas. You need to know as much as possible about the nature of dogs, about the breed as such and how to actually train a dog. Only when you know all this can you judge whether your goals are realistic or illusory, i.e. whether you and your Golden would actually be able to reach those goals.

> ⊃ Step 2: Get clear an concise

There is the saying that 'the longest journey begins with the first step'. Acting on the knowledge you gained and following the path in the direction of your goal is bound to give you the desired results. The clearer you are on where you want to get, the better and actionable your knowledge is and the more dedicated and committed you step out, the easier it will be for you to reach that place of happiness together with your Golden Retriever.

The Golden Retriever Education System will give you the knowledge and strategies to educate both yourself and your dog.

You can only teach your dog if and when you yourself have learned how to be a teacher for your dog.

There is one more noteworthy thing about the **Golden Retriever Education System.**

This is that unlike other systems it's goal is not a well trained dog; it's goal is to help you to *educate* your dog.

Here is the difference between a trained dog and a well educated dog:

▶ The trained dog does things because you tell him to.

▶ The educated dog does things because he wants to do them. He does not follow your orders as such but he has understood how you want him to behave and therefore he behaves in that way.

He has internalized your wishes as his rules and so he needs very few commands to follow. He complies with your wishes because your wishes are his wishes.

What do I mean by this?

Imagine being out in the park with your dog. You are having a conversation with another dog owner whilst your dog is playing with his dog. Now it is time to go. You call your dog.

The *trained* dog responds because he has learned that responding to your command is warranted. He comes because you have called him.

The *educated* dog stops playing and follows you because he understands that "We are going".

The educated dog does not jump up at people because he has understood that "We don't jump up at people". He does not need you there telling him what to do, he just behaves in a sensible way because that is who he is.

Whilst traditional training systems focus on obedience and submission the **Truth Based Golden Retriever Education System** supports the dog in developing his intelligence and own personality. Through a sound education he will learn how to behave in different circumstances and become able to deal with all sorts of different surroundings and people.

➲ Step 3: Put that knowledge and information into wise, loving and consistent action.

Over time he will become wise enough to be your trusted companion in 'all sorts of weather' and not just someone who is inferior to you and obeys your commands because he has to.

Of course training is a part of educating your dog, but his education does not stop there. You will need to expose him to a wide variety of people and places so he can gain the necessary experience and flexibility which are part of canine intelligence, but you need to tailor this to his emotional development. This is not something you do with your young puppy because he hasn't got the brain to deal with a great deal of variety yet. He needs to stay close to home for the first six month of his life because he needs it's familiarity to feel safe.

This is where many well meaning puppy parents and puppy trainers make massive mistakes.

By exposing youngsters to the noises and smells of a town or shopping mall or some crowded place they overwork his young nervous system and cause fear and stress inside of him.

Introducing new stimuli to a puppy is a delicate process which needs lots of care and consideration.

▶ You want to make sure you don't overwhelm him. As he gets older his nervous system and brain will be able to digest more and more stimuli.

▶ As this happens he will feel more secure in himself.

Being bigger the angle from which he sees the world changes, his view of the world literally increases and so he can slowly but surely make better use of his vision.

As this progresses he is getting himself ready to explore the world more and more and you can start taking him to new and more exciting places.

The early training you give him is not an end in and of it's own, it is the beginning of the education process because it teaches him the words of those commands he needs to know so he can go out there with you. The commands he knows and follows enable you to communicate your wishes to him which is an essential part of any friendship.

Even though this conceptual difference between training and educating your dog may seem a little complicated at first, it makes a huge difference when it comes to living life with an adult Retriever.

The **Truth Based Golden Retriever Parenting System** will help you bring up your precious and so much loved Golden puppy in harmony with his very nature. Only by understanding and respecting your pup's real nature can you create a life full of happiness for your puppy, yourself and your family. This is the Master Key to your happiness as a Golden Retriever owner.

Learn How To Use this Master Key Now!

Core Principles

Pleasure and Pain

➲ Pleasure versus pain.

All living beings work on the *Pleasure versus Pain* principle. All animals are hard- wired for pleasure. When we experience pleasure our bodies are flooded with pleasurable neurotransmitters which are beneficial and healthy.

Our bodies tolerate a certain amount of "pain chemicals", i.e. stress hormones for a limited time only. When the cells of our bodies are being "bathed" in those chemicals for too long they can become compromised over time.

Learning and growth are only possible under certain circumstances. The feeling of being safe and relaxed are paramount to learning, healing and growth.

Therefore we need to find ways to create as much pleasure and as little pain as possible for our youngster.

Your Personal Qualities As a Good Retriever Parent

➲ The 8 Virtues

The **8 Virtues** of a Golden Retriever Owner set the stage for healthy puppy development, while the **Ugly 4** greatly harm his mental, emotional and physical development.

➲ The virtues: PLEASURE

To remember the virtues easily just think of the word **PLEASURE**:

P   Patient

L   Loving

E   Empathic

A   Assertive

S   Safe

U   Unconditional

R   Reliable

E   Enthusiastic

➲ The ugly 4 : PAIN

And the Ugly 4 spell as **PAIN**:

P   Punishing

A   Angry

I   Impatient

N   Negative

As you set out on the task to be a very good dog parent you continuously need to review you own behaviour to ensure that the **UGLY 4** don't start running the show.

Since we are only human we can not avoid getting impatient or even angry. We are taught to believe in the benefits of at least small amounts of punishment and due to our personal obligations and life's requirements we will need to neglect our puppy at times.

To say that one never resorts to punishment or never gets angry or impatient would be just as dishonest as saying that one always cares for puppies' feelings and wants as much as one ought to do.

But we **can** *and* **must** make sure that we create as little pain in our youngster as possible by consciously taking charge of our actions and feelings and keeping our spirits as high as possible during those taxing first month with our new lifetime friend.

It is good to remember that dog training is an inside job and that ideally we lead your dogs with our inner strength rather than with any form of physical power.

Realities and Secrets

Puppy training and dog parenting rests on
3 Facts and 7 Core Secrets

⮑ 3 realities

The **3 Facts** are the truth **about** your *puppy* and her needs, her canine nature as well as her individual personality – *your* personal reality and the reality of your *lifestyle* and circumstances.

Your puppy's Truth

⮑ 1. Your pup's truth.

Your puppy is a young animal, *not a human being.* She is a member of the canine family and will be a grown dog one day. She is not a small dog but a baby dog. This means that she has special needs and wants and her development follows certain laws. Ignoring her needs or not catering for her special requirements will damage her mental, emotional and physical health. Her development will be more or less endangered. Behavioural problems and/or physical health issues become likely.

Your own personal reality

⮑ 2. Your own reality.

You are an adult human being with a *set personality.* You have your likes and dislikes, your strong points and your weaknesses. Your body is healthy and fit to a greater or lesser degree just as you are more or less assertive, patient or resourceful. The events of your life have shaped your emotions, thoughts, expectations. You have your own problems and coping strategies, your needs and wants. Your conscious and subconscious belief systems shape your behaviour and the trust you place in yourself and others.

You need to respect who you are and what you have become. Not all of us are emotionally or physically able to do the same things. If and when you expect too much from yourself you will become frustrated. It is important that you set up the circumstances of bringing up your puppy in a way that meets your capabilities.

Here is what I mean:

At the time of writing I am 56 years old and physically not the fittest person in the world. I need to take it slowly and respect the fact that my physical strength is limited. Taking my puppy Sweetheart outside to do her business all hours of the day and night would do me no good. So I have decided to take a slower route to housetraining young Sweetheart. I have set up a gigantic cat litter box and trained her to use this when she needs to go potty.

Fortunately her breeder had already taught the whole litter to use something like it from a very early age. By making use of the litter box training my puppy had already received and by expanding it to suit my requirements I was able to teach my puppy to be clean and at the same time spared myself the effort of carrying her outside in all sorts of weather.

Since dogs have a tendency to become clean anyway, Sweetheart soon used the box on a regular basis. After a while I put the box into the hall, still very accessible for her but not close to our living room or bedroom. She soon learned to go there whenever she needed to.

Now, at the age of seventeen weeks she is able to walk down the stairs to go into the garden and she needs to go toilet less often. She comes up and looks at me and I take her outside. We still have the box in case she needs to use it at night or when I am too busy to read her signs properly.

Of course I did not rely on the box in the way of not taking her outside when possible but I used the convenience of having it indoors to spare myself waiting outside for her to do her business on cold and windy nights or rainy days.

Had I not respected my own physical limitations I would have become more impatient with her progress and that would not have been good for either of us.

The reality of your life and circumstances

⊃ 3. The reality of your life and circumstances.

This include the place where you live and its location, whether it's in an urban or more rural setting, apartment or house, with neighbours close by or no one in sight. It's furnishing and immediate surroundings.

▶ Your lifestyle, whether you are a party animal with lots of friends and long nights out or lead more a quiet, secluded life.

▶ Your work and the hours they keep you from home. You may be living on your own or with a partner or family.

▶ Your finances and the amount of money you have to spend on your dog's keep and healthcare.

Whilst some settings make keeping and bringing up a Golden Retriever easier than others you need to optimize your conditions and fine tune them to bringing up your puppy.

Some friends of yours may not like dogs and thus not accept invitations as freely as before, some friends might even be phobic when it comes to dogs.

If that is the case you should not try to convince them otherwise because your pup will pick up on their rejection and they are bound to be more reserved towards her than would be good for the development of her trust towards humans.

When you are in a secluded, rural setting with houses few and far between you can allow your puppy to become more vocal than you would be able to allow her to be with neighbours close by. Allowing your dog to develop the habit of barking all the time is not such a good idea when you live in a flat or apartment either.

Since we live in a house with neighbours upstairs and downstairs I needed to restrict my four year old Sunshine's vocalisations as much as possible. He is one who enjoys a good barking session and expresses his happiness by rolling over on the floor barking. It was quite a task to stop him from doing this at home without intimidating him. When Sweetheart joined the household I had to teach her too that barking inside is not what we want.

If money is one of the subjects you worry about frequently you would be well advised to start a savings account for vet bills. Dog's medical needs can soon become very expensive and burn a deep hole into your pockets. When my dog Sebastian fell ill I had to spend close to 3500 Euros within a year! With a good savings account just for vet bills, paying for his treatments would have been a lot easier for me.

Here is the tip:

If creating a happy time for yourself and your puppy is what you want to do it might be a good idea to take a closer look at your own personal reality as well as taking a good look at the reality of your life and circumstances. Find possible challenges and look for solutions before they turn into problems. You have the right to adjust circumstances to your own needs and the needs of your baby dog. Remember that in those first month of his life with you, your pup ideally should meet only nice people and live in a happy family. His emotional well-being and character development depends on you being balanced and well. Therefore creating harmonious surroundings and circumstances for yourself and your puppy is of great importance.

The 7 core secrets

The 7 core secrets *Knowledge – Understanding – Patience – Clarity – Consistency – Trust and Love* are essential factors of each and every close relationship – be it with a dog, a horse or a fellow human being. The higher you score on each of the 7 Secrets the happier and healthier your relationships will be and the more successful you will feel in your entire life. Let's take a closer look at each of them in the context of parenting and educating your puppy:

Knowledge

The more you know about dogs and puppies the better – or at least that is what you'd expect. But you need to be careful because there is a lot of "expert knowledge" out there which will actually lead you down the wrong path.

Many people who call themselves dog experts actually perpetuate those myths that cause first time puppy parents to interpret their Golden's behaviour in the wrong way which again adds to their confusion. Make sure the knowledge you take in informs you of positive training methods and scientifically proven facts. You need some good present day knowledge about health care, feeding regimes and nutrition, about the temperament of the Golden Retriever and how to champion yours as well as some first aid techniques.

In order to really educate your wonderful puppy in sync with her needs and abilities it is paramount that you know some hard facts about the way your puppy's nervous systems work and how those nervous systems control behaviour and overall development. Failing that you are like a captain at sea who knows where he wants to go but has no idea of how to get there quickly and safely.

But since all mammals work under the same principles this kind of knowledge will also help you understand your own actions and feelings better, thereby empowering you to really create a successful relationship with your puppy.

I am a great believer in the power of knowledge. The knowledge I am going to share with you in this book will not only benefit you by helping you understand yourself and your puppy better, it will also help you do what needs to be done in a very efficient manner so that success with your puppy is inevitable.

➲ Your understanding

Understanding

This refers not only to your comprehension of the facts and how to apply them but also to your emotional understanding of your puppy, i.e. your empathy. When you understand how your puppy feels and why she reacts in a certain way in any given circumstance your reactions will be a lot more loving, supportive and effective then they would be if they were just reason driven.

➲ Your patience

Patience

Patience is the core value of all good teachers. You need to be patient when it comes to the development of your pup's house training issues, when it comes to her learning how to behave and how not to behave and so on and so forth. The *perfect puppy parent leads the way but allows the pup's development to set the time table.*

Clarity

➲ Your Clarity

In dog training as in any other communication clarity is key. When you express yourself in a mixed up and muddled up fashion no one is likely to understand you.

The problem is that our dogs watch our bodies and follow their messages rather than listening to our words. And the puppy is a complete stranger to our world so he needs us to be even clearer in our messaging.

Here comes the catch: People are often unaware that their bodies speak louder than their words! Please make sure that you express yourself in a way that your little one can understand – even if it means retraining yourself.

Consistency

⊃ Your consistency

Consistency paves the way to learning and understanding. Since learning means creating neural pathways in the brain we always have to follow through with our commands and messages.

The principle of consistency also refers to teaching your pup the meaning of your words and signs by always using the same ones to convey a meaning. This is how language is learned. Imagine learning a foreign language. Don't you have to rely on one word meaning the same thing all the time? If the German teacher for instance told you that a table is called "Tisch" in German and then called it "Schreibtisch" the next time and "Ablage" after that you would be more than confused and not be able to really learn the German word for table, would you? The same is true for your puppy and that is why consistency is such a key principle in puppy education.

Trust

⊃ Mutual
trust

Trust is the result of experience. Your puppy needs to learn that you are a good, reliable person who will always protect him. He also needs to establish trust in mankind in general and in himself.

The safe environment you create for him allows him to explore and get to know the world. The feeling of trust can only be developed through the absence of harm and pain. This is where your patience and reliability, your unconditional friendliness, gentleness as well as your clarity bear fruit.

On the other hand you need to trust yourself, your instincts, insights and your ability to lead the way so that you can eventually trust your dog.

Love

⊃ Your love

Even though our love should be unconditional, experience shows that we as humans tend to associate love with good and wanted behaviour. We find it hard to love a person or a dog who consistently frustrates us, ignores our wishes or violates our boundaries. A dog may have difficulties loving unstable, moody and unreliable people too, but in general dogs seem to love more unconditionally than humans.

This means that whilst your puppy adores you no matter what, you might find it just a little harder to keep that loving feeling active if your dog constantly misbehaves and generally gives you a hard time.

Essentially all love for someone else is closely related to self – love. The more you love yourself the more you will be able to love your dog or anyone else for that matter.

It is only by respecting your own dreams and desires that you will take your puppy raising ventures serious enough to succeed. Raising and educating a Golden takes time, dedication and effort.

In order to really find the time and put all other things aside for a while you need to allow yourself to value your dream. Really connecting with your heart's desire to make your dream of that wonderful relationship with your Golden come true is a lot easier when you love yourself.

Quick Recap:

The **3 Realities** set the stage for your and your puppy's life together whilst the **7 Core Pillars** determine the quality of that life. The degree to which those essential requirements are met decides whether it's going to be a happy time full of joy and fun or an unhappy sorrowful and bothersome journey. If they are in harmony your life with your Golden will be a harmonious one too.

Gathering present day knowledge, being understanding and patient, always expressing oneself clearly and always being consistent takes some doing. But doing it is *inevitable* because they are the soil on which trust and love can grow. Depending on your character and motivation they come easier or harder for you. Since these virtues are so important for the well being of your dog you need to train yourself to improve what's lacking.

One of the core messages of this book is that *dog training is an inside job*. By this I mean that you need to do your best to develop the mentioned qualities to become the person who walks his talk, who is fair and considerate and the authority figure a dog can look up to.

In order for our dogs to respect us we need to behave in a respectable way. We need to communicate clearly so our dogs can understand us and we need to be motivated to understand what our dogs are telling us. Friendship is a two way street and if we expect our puppies to learn how to be good dogs we must, in turn, strive to be good dog parents.

Your puppy thinks that these are the 7 secret keys to his heart

And this is what your puppy would like you to make of it all:

On Knowledge

⮡ Know me

Please gather true knowledge about me and don't believe what everybody says. Learn about my development and my brain because those decide my actions and how I behave.

Find ways to train me without hurting or upsetting me. Using rattling cans frightens me. Please don't train me through fear.

On Understanding

⮡ Understand me

Please try to see the world through my eyes. I am only tiny compared to you and all I see are legs. The world is vast for me. I don't understand you and I don't know what you want me to do.

My senses are not yet fully developed nor is my brain. They take their time to become fully functional. Until they are, I can not be obedient, I can not behave like a big dog and I need your protection and support.

Understand me and always give me the benefit of doubt. I never intend to test you or push your limits.

Whatever I do is governed by my instincts and due to my developmental stage. I don't do the things I do because I want to upset you, I do them because I don't have any choice yet.

Please never get angry with me for being who and what I am. Listen to your heart and you will be able to connect with me.

⊃ Be patient

On Patience

Please be patient with me! Understand that I am not yet able to control my digestion or my behaviour.

Please be patient when I don't do what you want me to do because I don't understand your language yet.

Please don't rush me into something I am not ready for – I am doing the best I can!

Please don't get angry because I am not yet ready to know what's wrong and what's right!

On Clarity

Please express yourself so that I can understand you.

Help me learn your language and what you mean.

I read your body more than your words because words have less meaning.

Please don't give me mixed up messages.

On Consistency

Show me what you want and reward me at once.

Stop me at once when I am going wrong.

My brain needs to make the connection and can only create patterns when the reward comes at once.

Never ever punish me some time after I have done something wrong.

Don't let me do tomorrow what I wasn't allowed to do today.

Don't let me do today what I am not supposed to do in a few weeks time.

⊃ Trust me so I can trust in you

On Trust

Be trustworthy.

Protect me.

Keep me safe.

Help me learn to trust you by not shouting at me or hurting me

Don't throw things at me.

Trust in my ability to develop and learn over time.

Trust in yourself because I need you to teach me the right things.

⊃ Love me

On Love

Love me.

Always and no matter what I do.

Tell me often that you love me.
Look at me with loving eyes.

Talk about my good points, never about my mistakes.

Allow me to love and adore you.

Allow me to be near you.

Love yourself.

Love is more than a feeling, more than an emotion. Love delivers.

As dog owners we express our love and respect for our dogs by educating and training them on How To Be Good Dog Citizens.

➲ Conclusions

Not to train them means subjecting them to a life full of restraint and frustration. It means subjecting ourselves to many years of stress and dissatisfaction and to create a relationship dominated by blame and worry.

Both you and your Golden Retriever deserve a happy relationship, one that nourishes both of you and gives you the feeling of deep and sincere friendship.

I know that you love your puppy and that you want him to be the happiest puppy in the world. This is my deep and sincere wish for him too.

Because I love our Goldens with all my heart I have developed the **Truth Based Education System** which is completely free from using any kind of punishment or unkindness towards your youngster. I know that you would hate to punish or frighten your puppy in the process of training and educating him but I also know that there are many training modalities out there counting on emotional force and pain. I understand that this may be a reason why so many gentle and loving owners shy away from training their puppies or adults.

But it does not have to be like that at all!

By respecting your *own personal* reality and also the *reality of your life and circumstances* and adjusting them carefully to your puppy's needs, as well as respecting your *baby's truth* you set the stage for her sound development.

By gaining present day **knowledge** and **understanding** which translate into an appropriate amount of **patience** and by training yourself to ALWAYS be **clear** and **consistent** you put down the foundations for mutual trust and love.

Avoiding the "**5 I's**" – *impatience, inconsistency, insensitivity, irrationality* and even *insecurity* will become quite easy and finally you will be able to train your puppy under the "*all PLEASURE no PAIN*" principle.

Because you will embody the **8 virtues** of a successful dog owner which are:

Patience, Love, Empathy, Assertiveness, Softness, Unconditional Reliability and *Enthusiasm.* And the **Ugly 4** Punishment, Anger, Impatience and Negativity will cause your puppy *no* PAIN because you will have learnt how to train her without it.

How to Create Lasting Happiness for You and Your Golden

Daddy will always be there for you!

Happiness Questions

⊃ Asking yourself

Get into the habit of asking yourself some helpful questions because the questions you ask yourself give guidance to your actions.

Since it is your goal to create a wonderful, happy life experience both for yourself and your Golden Retriever puppy, why not try these?

▶ Would I like to be my own dog?

▶ Would I choose to live with me if I had the choice?

▶ And would I like to be my own puppy?

▶ If yes, why?

▶ If no, why not?

▶ If I was my dog how would I like to be treated and educated?

▶ If I was my dog what would I need most to be really happy?

Here are the **3 Core Questions** we really need to ask ourselves as we bring up our puppies – in fact those are the questions we need to reflect upon during our Golden's entire lifetime:

▶ Am I loving?

▶ Am I consistent?

▶ Am I acting wisely?

⊃ Am i loving?
⊃ Am I consistent?
⊃ Am i acting wisely

Instead of acting wisely and in agreement with our goals we find that quite often our reactions are based on automatic emotional responses.

Here is what I mean:

The puppy squats and piddles on the carpet – we feel the surge of anger rising. But we check ourselves by reminding us that he is not house trained yet. We start house training him, taking him outside in all sorts of weather and in the middle of the night. He performs at once – we are happy because we can rush back in. He takes his time – we get impatient.

He does something else and does not perform at all – we get annoyed. After twenty minutes in the cold we go back in. Useless puppy!

Two minutes later he piddles on the carpet! We get angry. Why the heck didn't he do that out there just a minute ago?! The same thing happens three times in a row. Sometimes he performs outside at once, sometimes after a short while, sometimes he takes his time. As long as he does it outside and within a reasonable time frame we are happy.

But when he doesn't do it outside at all and on the carpet instead, we feel angry and frustrated. And then one day, right out of the blue our fuses blow!

How would you feel if you were in your puppy's place in such a situation?

⊃ Put yourself in your puppy's place.

Changing our perspective helps us fine tune our behaviours so they meet our own standards.

Let's take a closer look at the **3 Core Questions**.

Question No. 1: Am I loving?

You will know whether an action of yours is loving when you ask yourself, how much loved would I feel if this – your – action was done to me.

⊃ Question #1: Am I loving?

How loved would I feel if I were subjected to that treatment?

Dogs have feelings just like we have because we share the same mammalian brains. Therefore this question can be a useful guideline for you.

But wait! There is one thing to bear in mind:

What feels loving at the moment might not feel loving at all when it comes to long-term effects.

What I mean is this: Your pup will certainly feel loved when you feed her great amounts of those lovely tidbits – but what is going to happen over time?

John was such a victim of "loving" behaviour. His master was a great believer in the sentence "Love goes through the stomach". He shared all his food with the puppy. Whatever he ate, John got his share …. It seemed that cream cakes were John's favourites and so he was allowed to enjoy plenty of them.

When I met John he was two years old, could hardly move, in short: he was a barrel on legs. His life was a sad one, since he was unable to play or even run. So how loving had his owner really been?

There is another kind of lovingness which produces harm in the long run. It is called *permissiveness and it sounds like this:* "Oh, just let her chew those slippers. There is no harm in that. They are old anyway…. " "Oh, just let her jump up at yourself. She is soooo happy to see you!"

These sentences reveal the belief that teaching rules is unloving. The secret is this: Rules need to be taught right from the word "Go" – but in an absolutely loving and gentle, age-related style. It is not so much about the content. It is about *packaging and delivery.*

⊃ Here's the secret.

When The Dog Trainers Advice Gets In The Way Of Love

What do you think of the following puppy training tip some expert gave a lady first-time owner:

▶ When the puppy comes up to you because it wants to be stroked and cuddled. Don't. If you will do what the pup wants, you will only teach the dog in the making that he is boss and that you are servant. Never allow puppy on any furniture and always eat before you feed the puppy. Make sure he sees you eating. That way you establish your leadership right from the start.

▶ Never allow your dog to lick you under any circumstances. This will make him give his bugs to you (this was sound advice from owner's mother).

What do you think came from this?

When I was called in to solve the pup's car sickness problem – which I did by the way – I was greeted by the most wonderful loving youngster- 9 months old. He lavished me with all the love and attention his young heart could give. I felt wonderful!

The odd one out was his "mummy". Looking rather sad and lost, she felt left out and unhappy. Not knowing what was going on, I asked her about it.

She told me that her pup played with everyone, sharing love and joy with her husband and kids… everyone but her! She was clearly hurt and very confused about this. "He doesn't love me – there must be something wrong with me" was her painful conclusion. This sounded so unbelievable that I asked her if she had abused him physically at any time? No. Had she shouted at him frequently? No.

So what on earth had she done to inhibit her pup's affection?

She told me how she had raised him and said: "Of course I made sure that I was the one who initiated and ended all physical contact.

That I never cuddled with him *when he wanted* me to.

I did all the right things to make sure he didn't become dominant over me…"

Wait a minute, you did WHAT?

She had a dog trainer in when the pup was very young. She had wanted to do all the right things right from the start. It had not been easy for her to refuse her pup's love and attention – in fact it had been very painful, but she did it anyway.

With all this rejection going on, her pup had turned away from her with the conclusion that "there must be something wrong with me – she does not like me!" and luckily found more loving companionship with the husband and kids of the family.

Since the dog's heart is very forgiving and the brain is always out for gain, we managed to turn things around within a few coaching sessions. And the two of them are now a very happy pair, just like of both of them had intended it to be right for the start.

Lesson: Your heart knows how to treat a puppy when it comes to showing your affection. No matter what "they" say. Trust yourself.

➲ Question
#2: Am I
consistent?

Question No. 2: Am I consistent?

Helpful sub-questions: Do I walk my talk? Do I mean what I say? Am I always using the same words and commands?

Or do I confuse my puppy and actually prevent the creation of neural pathways and habits in the brain by: saying NO! and letting her do it anyway? Calling her to come to me and then jump to answer the telephone? Forbidding her to do something or go somewhere one day and allowing or even encouraging her to do actually that same thing next day? Do I praise her for being a good girl when I am in a good mood, but ignore her efforts when I am in a bad mood?

Many years ago, when I was still taking in Goldens to train them because their owners couldn't, I worked with a wonderful but grossly overweight young bitch, call her Jane. Jane had gotten into the habit of pulling on the lead like an excavator, nose down and off she went like mad. Another thing was that she was for ever begging to get food from the table, even stealing it when no one was looking. Jane was unruly, disobedient and not nice to live with. But she had a Golden heart and was willing to learn.

So my husband and I worked very hard to teach her the ways of a well behaved dog citizen, spending countless hours with heelwork and doing our best to discourage her from stealing food off the table.

At the end of three month Jane walked to heel, lay under the table during our meal times without begging and had completely dropped her food stealing habits. Those were the things the owners had asked us to achieve for her and by being very consistent the three of us had succeeded!

Then came the day to return her to her owners. In long telephone conversations I had explained how they would need to behave in future. They were never ever to feed her off the table again or share their food with her during mealtimes. To this they agreed and expressed their happiness because that problem had been solved so well.

After a happy greeting we decided to go to a coffee shop to celebrate their reunion. As we sat at the table having our cakes Jane lay on the floor looking up at her owner. Jane wasn't begging, she was just looking, happy to be with her mummy again.

⮑ Remember what you read about **consistency** on pp. 79 and 87? Here's how not to do it.

"No", my client said to her dog, "**you are not having any cake.**" Jane kept just looking at her.

Then, to my amazement and bitter frustration my client said, much to herself: "Oh well then, if you must, have a piece of cake!" And with that she gave her dog a piece of cream cake! I could have screamed at her but obviously didn't. When I asked the obvious "Why?" the lady replied: "Oh Martina, it was just a small piece, surely that won't do her any harm! Now she isn't **begging** any more I think it is okay if I give her a little reward".

During that meeting my client and her husband displayed such complete and utter inconsistency that I knew that all our efforts had been in vain. I still feel sorry for Jane today because her owners trained her to be a nuisance whilst blaming her for her unruly behaviour at the same time. That dog just couldn't win!

The importance of consistency will reveal itself further when we get to the section on how puppies learn.

Question No. 3: Am I acting wisely?

⮩ Question #3: Am I acting wisely?

"There is acting and acting wisely. Acting gives you the feeling of having done something. Acting wisely leads to your success." These strange sounding sentences were given to me as insights during the deep meditation I once did before a seminar I was about to teach to a group of Golden Retriever owners under the headline of: "New Ways into Happiness".

Of course, yes! This is such a true statement and you can apply it to all walks of life. Acting wisely gets you closer to your goals. Whilst acting out of the need to do something gives you mixed results. This really sums up the first two questions as well. Here is what I mean:

If you really want that loving, happy and reliable relationship with your Golden Retriever then doing things which potentially damage his trust in you and in the world in general, might not be such a good idea. Even if and when he pees and poos on your carpet or ruins that expensive silk scarf. Sound temperament comes through a balanced nervous system and a properly working limbic system. A healthy digestive tract and a properly working immune system are the prerequisites of a healthy body and need good food and nourishment.

Love comes through the positive bonds we create. And the bonds we create need the time we spend together in a pleasurable bonding way. So when we make sure to provide all the good things for body and soul and leave out the bad things we are well on our way to giving our puppy a good healthy start for a happy life.

➲ Wisdom versus fashion.

Unfortunately there is a great gap between wisdom and fashion.

The right things to do are often those which are not the most comfortable ones. They come with a certain amount of effort and work. Bringing up a Golden Retriever puppy means having to leave the comfort zone of your daily life as a non-dog owner. You will have to make amends. You will have to invest time and energy. You will need to make your puppy a priority. But the rewards for all those efforts will be unbelievable and you will have lots of fun doing it!

The first six months of your pup's life are full of excitement, growth and learning for both of you! This is a fantastic time and you can make the best of it! Enjoy the NOW and set the stage for a wonderful future!

> **Remember:** Learn how to be loving, how to be consistent and how to act wisely. By learning this you will able to create a fantastic, happy life experience not only for your dog – but also for yourself in all areas of your life.

Even if you don't feel loving at times and even if it is hard for you to be consistent and you don't see how you can be wise – just put on an act. Habits and abilities are created by doing.

↪ About habits and abilities.

▶ *You can train yourself* to keep your not so loving feelings at bay and never act on them.

▶ *You can learn how to be consistent* if you just watch and correct yourself.

▶ And *you can learn to structure your habits* so that your habits are in accordance with your overall goals.

▶ *You can reach your goals* but you can't reach them by sitting on your sofa watching TV.

▶ *You can create that wonderful relationship* with your *dog and* *he can learn all those* *things you want him to know with ease.*

Secret Steps Into Happiness

Shere joy and happiness

⊃ Setting
goals.

Setting goals for yourself and your Golden

You know how so many people complain about their dogs one way or another. How they are never really satisfied with their pooches' actions and behaviours? He is pulling on the lead, she is barking day and night, he doesn't come when called, she chews the carpets, he doesn't get into the car, she doesn't like children, he is impossible to show, she doesn't retrieve properly – the list is endless, isn't it?

How come so many people are so unhappy with their dogs even though they had raised them themselves?

I guess it is because they never made a plan and didn't follow any guidelines because they didn't have any plans for their life as a dog owner.

Reflecting on the question of what you want to do with your dog, how you want to spend time together and what you would like to achieve almost never crosses first time owner's minds. Even many of the more experienced ones don't think about dog parenting as something in which goals should ever be considered.

Many people just get a dog because they happen to want one or maybe to please their kids.

That's exactly what my parents did, when I, age 14 began to pester them because I wanted a dog. They decided to be loving parents and off we went to the local animal shelter where we fell for the sad eyes of a two year old Dalmatian male. Little did they know that we headed for trouble! Not only was he a severely traumatized chap but also extremely uneducated. In those days one did not think much about dog training or the emotions of a dog. Way back in 1972 people were concerned about other things.

But it seems that things have not really changed in the way that dog owners create a vision of their lives with their dogs. They just get one, go to classes and wonder why beloved doggy creates such problems in daily life.

Don't make this mistake!

Ask yourself how you want your life to be when your Golden puppy has grown up.

What do you want to do?

Is she just going to be your companion who goes for long walks with you? Are you going to travel with her? Are you going to walk her in fields or in the forests?

Or are you interested in any kind of sporting events like Agility or Obedience competitions? Do you perhaps want to show her?

How do you envision his overall behaviour? More of the obedient type or rather pleasing himself and only doing what you say when he feels like it?

How do you want him to interact with other dogs? Playing with them, ignoring them or fearfully avoiding or intimidating them?

Do you want him to pull you along country lanes or walk next to you without a lead?

How many hours do you expect him to be able to spend on his own?

Do you hope he will come to the whistle and come when called?

How would you like him to behave at home? Guard the property by barking at everyone in sight? Jumping up at your guests giving them the sloppy treatment? Or the muddy paw decoration all over their nice clean suits?

Why do I ask you all these questions?

Because the choice is yours! You get to decide which way your life as a Golden Retriever parent is going. You have the power and the responsibility to create the best life possible for both yourself and that wonderful, loving puppy of yours who will, in the not so distant future be your adult Golden Retriever.

Here is what you can do right now:

Step 1

Sit down in a quiet place, turn off your phone and internet, make sure no one is going to disturb you for at least 30 minutes. Get a pen and some paper and sit down on your most comfortable chair.

⊃ 1st step - take a breath

Close your eyes and relax. Focus on your breathing, watch your breath come and go – allow your mind to become very quiet.

As you just sit there thoughts will come to you – just imagine them walking past, don't pay any attention to any of them.

Just relax.

Imagine a place in which everything is possible. This space is safe and secure.

When you feel at ease and nicely relaxed travel into the future.

See yourself with your Golden – watch the pair of you walk along the path of life.

Ask yourself: What would really, really make both of us happy?

Watch your dog do all the things you would like him to do and allow yourself to experience the pleasure of your joint activities.

Stay in that state for as long as you wish. When you return, write down what you experienced and after that make sure you return to your normal state.

Over the next few days keep asking yourself "What would really, really make both of us happy?"

Make sure you only allow yourself to dwell on positive thoughts, after all you are planning a wonderful life together and not a mutual nightmare.

The clearer you can see yourself with your pet in a state of happiness the easier you will find creating lots of opportunities to be happy together.

Step 2

⮩ 2nd step - define your goals.

Create a list of goals which will help you and your Golden along the path.

The list may look like this:

I would like my Thomas to

▶ come to the whistle

▶ walk on the lead in a relaxed manner

▶ fetch a ball or even a dummy when I ask him to do so

▶ get on with other male dogs

▶ be calm and collected when we are out together

▶ accompany me on my weekly trip to the city centre

▶ go to work with me and relax in the office

▶ allow me to show him at dog shows and behave wonderfully in the ring

▶ feel safe around people in and outside our home

▶ feel safe and relaxed when we are with other dogs

▶ jump into the car and enjoy his rides

I don't want him to

▶ jump up at me when I come home

▶ chase the cat

▶ steel food from the table

▶ ignore me when we are out on walks and please himself

▶ pee on our neighbours gate post

▶ dig holes

This example list clearly shows you those behaviours which you must encourage by rewarding them and behaviours which you inhibit by telling him not to perform them or by correcting him when he does perform them.

It also offers you guidance for your own education:

If you see yourself relaxing with your pooch – what do you need to do in order to relax?

What traits and behavioural patterns must *you* develop or inhibit within yourself so you can be the owner of that wonderful dog? So that you can teach him all the good habits and help him mature into that relaxed, self confident, resilient adult Golden Retriever you envision him to be?

The truth is:

If you don't know where you're heading, it is not very likely that you'll ever get there.

Without a proper map it is hard to find the right way but when you don't have a destination it is even harder.

Most people say they want to be happy with life in general or with their dog in particular. They have long lists of "What nots" but often have no clue of the things they really want. Being negative seems to be easier than creating a blueprint for happiness.

⮡ A pitfall to bear in mind

Don't fall into that negativity trap with your puppy! A dog's life is too short to spend it troubleshooting. Rather become clear on your exact wishes and take the right steps to get there!

Your puppy wants you to be happy – if you're happy he will be happy.

The reason for this is that our dogs are such sensitive beings that they share our feelings. So when you are unhappy, your dog can not be happy.

Your unhappiness projects itself outwards by the way you smell, move, speak and act. Even by the energy you send outwards. A nervous, distressed or depressed person is not at all patient or loving and may be even be bad tempered. No fun to be with for anyone!

When you are distressed, worried, frustrated, anxious your system runs in survival mode, your body is dominated by stress hormones. Sooner or later your puppy will pick up on that and his body will also switch to survival mode with stress hormone levels elevating. This sets the stage for all sorts of problems.

So, to emphasize this point: your happiness is a vital factor for your dog's well-being too.

Step 3

Practice mentally to become that wonderful person your pup deserves you to be.

⮕ 3rd step - Become that wondeful person your pup deserves you to be.

The science of sport psychology has revealed to us that we are able to change our behaviour and become more proficient at some task either by training in a physical or in a **mental** way. Countless studies show that one works as well as the other. So in your quest to become a wonderful dog parent who does all the right things you can rely on your mind power.

You can actually use your imagination to create the blueprint for happiness.

Here is how you do it

Sit in a quiet place again, make sure no one disturbs you, turn off phone and the computer.

Your first assignment is to implement the habit of rewarding your puppy each and every time he does what you ask him to do.

⮕ See yourself rewarding your pup.

The reward has to follow the action at once and it needs to be given every time the desired behaviour is shown.

Most people can't manage this. They delay the reward for too long or simply forget all about it. This leads to the inevitable result that the desired behaviour is not learned.

Now imagine wanting to teach your puppy to SIT every time you raise the index finger of your left hand, saying SIT calmly and quietly.

See yourself and your puppy in front of your inner eye. Watch yourself saying "SIT" whilst raising your index finger. As the puppy sits down you IMMEDIATELY say: "Good girl!" and give her a small tidbit.

All this happens almost simultaneously: SIT + raised index finger + GOOD GIRL + tidbit.
Mentally rehearse this for several days. See and feel yourself doing it over and over again.

By doing this you create new neural pathways in your brain. Handing out the reward **immediately** after your pup has complied to your wish becomes a habit and as such an automatism.

You must train yourself before you can train your dog!

Now tackle something a bit more difficult.

Imagine you don't want your pup to jump up at you. This is so difficult because when she is so small and sweet bending down and petting her is an automatic response already. But when you don't want her to learn that jumping up at people is a good thing to do you should **not** pet her when she does so.

Now, in your mind's eye see her jumping up at you and you taking no notice of her efforts. Instead see yourself as you turn your body slightly sideways so that she has to put her front feet back onto the ground. As you do this you utter a short: "no!" in a calm but not enthusiastic way, using a deeper tone of voice.

Notice that it's not a NO! which would indicate a loud voice. You don't want a loud voice, just a short quiet message is enough to impress her.

Now see and feel yourself doing this each and every time she jumps up.

The secret lies in feeling yourself doing it. When you *feel* that you are doing something you really engage all the neural resources necessary for the intended action.

This fantastic technique will serve you no end if you really take the time to practice in that way before you actually begin teaching your puppy those commands you want him to follow later on.

Now that you have set your goals and learned a simple strategy of How To teach yourself to teach your puppy by always rewarding him for doing the right things, you are ready to take a closer look at the most important person of it all, i.e. your Golden Retriever puppy.

Let's discover sound, scientifically proven facts which lay the foundations for all those decisions you are going to make on her behalf.

Even though you may find some of this a bit overwhelming you need not worry because I am going to break it down in some easy-to-digest pieces of information so that you can integrate the new knowledge easily into your own wisdom bank.

Golden Retriever Puppy Life Facts

I promise to make you happy

Puppy Facts

When your precious little puppy came into your house and home he had no expectations whatsoever.

He didn't know about the preparations made for his arrival, had no idea about all the plans you made for his life at your place and certainly no clue of all the expectations running wild in your mind.

He had only one question: *"Will I be safe here or will I get eaten?"* All the new things and people he met in those first few days evoked just one internal response:

"Am I safe here or is my life in danger?"

Even though it may not have looked like it, his physiology was running on an overdose of stress hormones because he was in survival mode. The loss of his mother and siblings as well as the surroundings he had spent his first seven to eight weeks in totally blew his little mind.

A puppy is always asking the humans he encounters:

▶ Who are you and who am I in relationship to you?

▶ What is our relationship?

▶ Is it okay if I basically trust you or would it be safer to basically fear you?

Here are the most basic questions the young puppy tries to answer:

▶ How do I stay alive?

▶ How do I get food and shelter?

▶ How can I get what I want and need?

▶ How do I need to behave in order to avoid pain and gain pleasure?

▶ How can I cope with whatever life hands out to me?

In the early stages of his life your puppy develops rapidly. What is learned and created now makes up the templates of the mind and body. This is the reason why you want to take special care when it comes to your pup's *emotional experiences as well as his nutrition and health care.*

The early stages are the formative stages of our lives. This is just as true for your Golden Retriever as it is true for you and me.

Puppy Brain Development

*Understand my development and I
will be the best dog ever! Promised!*

To this day very little is known about the human brain and the way it works. Knowledge about brain development is still in its infancy. Even though neurobiologists and neuropsychologists are learning more about the brain as their instruments become more and more advanced it is going to take quite a while before all this new knowledge will become common wisdom.

What we do know by now is that the brain needs time to mature and grow and that some very important centres are not fully functional before the age of 24!

The parts of the brain we are talking about here are the ones which enable us to exercise complete control our actions and behaviours. The fact that those parts of the brain are not fully functioning before a person is in her twenties explains why young people behave as they do – seemingly unreasonable and sometimes even out of control.

What is true for humans is also true for dogs. The dog's brain needs time to grow and mature until all it's parts function fully.

And it might just be that the parts which make self control possible are also not fully usable before the dog reaches the beginning of adulthood.

Your dog needs to be able to exercise self control to the degree of not following his own impulses each and every time, to resist temptations just like we need to be able to control ourselves and resist temptations.

In order to follow *your* wishes your dog needs to suppress his own personal interests and keep his impulses at bay.

⊃ Your pup simply can't meet your expectations until his brain has reached a certain development stage.

When you expect him to reliably obey your commands like "Come" or "Stay" or even want him not to jump up at you with joy before he has reached that crucial brain development stage you are creating problems for yourself and for him.

He will just not be able to do what you expect reliably because his brain isn't ready for it yet. If you don't take this fact into account you will in the long run feel frustrated and may either resign or try to solve the problem with some harsher methods.

The latter will teach him to be afraid of you and will sow the seeds of mistrust towards you and people in general in his psyche.

Either way both of you are going to lose.

On the other hand, if you bear in mind that he can't do what he can't do and respect that it needs time for brains to become fully functional you can teach him little commands and rejoice in him learning them. At the same time you admire him for doing his best and honour the fact that he is too young to be good all the time.

▶ Ask yourself, how many times you tried to change your ways.

▶ Ask yourself how good you are at resisting temptations now and how good you were at it as a teenager or even child.

▶ Then, re-evaluate your expectations and set more realistic tasks for your puppy and yourself.

Brain development takes a long time and I found that a Golden is fully mature at the age of five. This is just my personal conclusion which I reached after forty years of studying the development of many Golden Retrievers. Give or take a year, it really does not matter all that much, does it?

The important thing is that we as our dog's guardians must never expect too much to early and always give our dogs the benefit of the doubt.

The Challenges

There are three areas of being with a puppy most new puppy owners find very difficult. Let's take a closer look at each one of them. They revolve around:

▶ When is my puppy clean in the house and how can I train him to go to the toilet outside?

▶ When can I leave my puppy on his own and how do I teach him to be on his own?

▶ When can I start training my puppy?

One other, even more important question is often overlooked:

▶ How can I bond with my puppy and how can I create a really deep relationship with her?

The answers you find to those fundamental questions determine how much your puppy is going to trust you and how his whole relationship with the world is going to be.

So let's address them one after the other.

Toilet Training

You may *start* with toilet training right on the first day but you must not expect lasting results straight away! Let's do some Q and A on the matter.

Tips On How To Toilet Train Your Puppy

Q: Which is the best way to toilet train my new Golden Retriever puppy? I just can't wait for him to do his business outside!

A: Okay, think of it this way: How soon would you expect a little baby girl to go to the toilet instead of using diapers? Are you having me on?

A: No, nothing could be further from the truth! I am just trying to make you see that your puppy is a little baby and can not be expected to be clean in the house in an instant.

Q: Which means what?

A: It means that you need to be patient and give your baby some time to develop sphincter muscle control which is a gradual process. Without proper control over his sphincter muscles he can not delay doing his business for any length of time once he has felt the urge to do so.

Because your pup needs to relieve himself within short intervals you should take him out:

1. once every two hours
2. before his meals and immediately afterwards
3. during and right after play
4. every time he wakes up

Q: But I am not always able to run when my puppy needs to go to the toilet. Surely he will be able to wait a minute or two:

A: I am sorry but a young puppy can not wait for us to put on our shoes and coat so we don't get wet outside. When a puppy needs to do his business it is always **"NOW!"**. One way out can be what is called "paper training". Many breeders initially educate their puppies to use a piece of paper or puppy toilet pads. That way the floor stays clean. If your pup was paper trained by his breeder all you need to do is put some newspaper on the floor and watch your baby piddle on it. Instead of using newspaper which is not really optimal because it gives off black colour and chemicals you could use a puppy toilet pad or two. Should your pup not be paper trained you could put him on the paper every time he sits down to do something. That way he will soon associate the two and start using the paper.

Either way, as your toilet training progresses you can move the paper closer and closer to the door so that when he needs to wee he will walk up to the door. As you notice this you can take him outside. Your puppy isn't being naughty when he does his business inside: He is simply not able to exercise proper control over his sphincter muscles or his bladder constrictor due to the development of his nervous system.

And he does *not know* that he needs to go to the toilet outside. This is something you need to teach him.

Q: But how can I teach him when I don't know that he needs to go outside?

A: Look out for these signs:

▶ puppy walks around as if he is trying to find a good spot
▶ puppy turns in a small circle
▶ puppy arches his back
▶ puppy walks around and squats down

As your puppy starts to understand that he needs to do his business outside he will start to look for the door or even walk up to it.

It is very important that you take him outside the very moment you see those signs! Your puppy will soon be able to do his big business outside but still needs patience with his piddles. This is a natural process.

Given time and attention your pup will not take long to be clean in the house but you need to expect "accidents" to happen. When getting excited or feeling submissive he or she might still do a pee inside. This is normal for young canines and you should not be angry about it. Canines hate to foul in their den so you can expect your puppy to do his best to keep his environment clean.

This is the reason why she will soon piddle in one of the rooms she doesn't stay in very often. Make sure to keep your puppy with you and don't let her have the freedom of the house before she is properly toilet trained.

⮌ Accidents will happen. Out of joy, out of excitment, out of fear. Keep calm, don't growl.

Q: Is that all there is to it? Sounds easy enough!

A: Yes, that's all. All you need is some patience and willingness to go outside whenever your pup needs to do something. Over the years I have found humour to be a great asset.

After all, is it really the end of the world to have some puppy pee on the carpet? Please be patient and supportive when it comes to toilet training and don't get angry with your pup if things take longer than expected. Every Golden is unique and sometimes things take as long as they take.

⊃ Leaving your puppy alone

Leaving your puppy home alone

When can you leave your puppy on his own and how can you teach him to be on his own?

One of the major problems puppy parents face is the fact that a young puppy needs them so much they can never leave him for any length of time. This makes the first few months of being a Golden Retriever owner quite difficult and in a way unpleasant.

You can't go anywhere without the puppy and you can't take him anywhere due to the fact that his immune system isn't ready to fight Parvovirus, Distemper or any other of those dangerous infections a dog can get before him having completed his course of inoculations which is usually not before the age of sixteen to eighteen weeks.

At the time of writing I am firmly in the hands of my wonderful puppy. She is now 16 weeks old, right in the middle of her teething stage and needs me like nothing else in the world.

Luckily I can take her out for some shorter walks during the day and she loves being in the car. I am fortunate enough to have another one who is four years old so I can leave her in the car with him for some time.

But I know how it feels when you are stuck inside the house! I find this the most troublesome time of the whole experience and I will be happy when she is old enough to start taking her along more often. I am also looking forward to the days when I can leave both of them on their own and go shopping again without needing someone in the house to look after her. But this is the "music of the future" because we ain't there yet by a long way.

I take this stage extremely seriously because I know from clients' experience and also through my studies what can happen when you rush things and leave your puppy on his own too soon.

Due to the *importance* of this subject I am going to take some time over answering the simple sounding question of "when can I leave her on her own".

Lets take a look at the pitfalls first:

⊃ Sepera-
tion anxiety

Separation Anxiety

Separation anxiety is an emotional problem that is afflicting more and more dogs and their owners! It seems to be one of the menaces of modern day dog ownership.

How so and why?

Dogs of all breeds and all sizes can suffer from severe stress when their owners leave them on their own for any length of time. When the dog parent leaves, the anxious dog 's sympathetic nervous system immediately takes over, the amygdala, the alarm system in the brain immediately starts working and as a result the body is flooded with stress hormones such as adrenalin and cortisol. Those cause all the symptoms of distress that we know from dogs that suffer from separation anxiety.

⊃ The
symptoms
of separation
anxiety range
from running
around to
self-mutilation

These symptoms vary from simple running around and panting to whining and barking, to destroying furniture, cushions, clothing, to self-mutilation which means licking the own body or scratching or biting oneself.

The dog is doing all these things in order to lessen the distress, to calm himself. One of the first mechanisms to get rid of stress hormones is to start some kind of movement because by moving around we reduce stress hormones. When the body is flooded with those hormones, it is in survival mode which means that the blood is going to the heart, to the muscles, but the blood is not going into the digestive system anymore and the brain works in a different way than it normally does.

Survival mode means that the body is ready to either fight, flee or freeze – hence the redistribution of oxygene and blood throughout the system.

Whilst separation anxiety is an extremely unpleasant condition for dog and owner alike, it is also a very, very difficult condition to actually treat and correct.

What causes separation anxiety?

The answer is quite simple: separation anxiety can be caused by the dog having been exposed to times of loneliness at too young an age or not having been taught to be on his own at all. Either way the following takes place when the dog is being left on his own:

The emotional side of being left behind from a puppy's perspective

This young puppy was too young to cope with being left on his own when his mummy went out shopping. He got frightened and his sympathetic nervous system took over which made him feel very unwell, restless and emotionally sick. No one was there to help him calm down again and relax into a state of security so his fear got worse and worse. He didn't know what to do, AND couldn't cope with the fear that someone was going to come and eat him.

He himself had no say in the matter, couldn't influence the way his emotions were heading. It was Nature's survival programme which caused him to suffer all the emotional and most likely physical pain, the nausea of being scared to death. His little heart was racing, blood rushing to his head. He needed to wee urgently. So he cried and cried and when no mummy came he started running around, feeling in a panic and utter state of despair. As time went by he got exhausted, finally fell asleep. When he awoke he was still on his own! The whole circle started all over again.

Finally, after what seemed to have been a life time, he heard the key turn in the lock! Thank God, mummy was back!

He rushed to the door, tried to get as close to her as possible but she took little notice because her hands were full. She shouted No! And pushed him away. He took no notice, tried even harder to get to her face so he could lick and show her how much he had missed her.

As soon as she saw that he had weed on the floor and pulled down things from all over the place her voice became cold and hard. Bad boy! Go away, you bad, bad puppy! Even so he didn't know what her words meant he felt her anger. What could he do to calm her again?

Now he was frightened of her but that was not as terrible as what he had gone through when she was away. And, after some time, the storm cleared away and mummy was nice and soft again. Happiness at last!

The next day brought the same pain. She went away and he felt overwhelmed by panic and fear.

His body hurt with all the tension building up inside and he found some relief in running around. Tearing at the curtains had a calming effect on the surge of stress hormones so he felt a little better.

This time she didn't stay away for such a long time, but when she came back she got very angry. If he only knew why? Why was she shouting and why was she as cold as ice for such a long time afterwards? At least she was back and she surely wouldn't kill him – or would she after all?

That evening saw the arrival of something very daunting and strange. It was shiny and looked like nothing he had ever seen before. Would it bite him? But Daddy and Mummy encouraged him to have a look. They smelt calm and seemed to be happy, so he overcame his initial apprehension and took a closer sniff. Then he felt a push and found himself inside the thing. Ugh!

Being a brave little dog he didn't cry, just sat there. They gave him something to eat whilst he was inside the thing and he felt sort of okay.

This went on for some days and then, one day, he couldn't get out anymore!

What was that?

His heart began to race, he started panting. He cried, he fought but he just couldn't get out. As the stress hormones took over he couldn't run around to get rid of them. He instinctively knew he was in severe danger because he couldn't run but there was nothing he could do about it! So the vagus nerve took over in his autonomic nervous system which caused him to just lay there in a state of shock. He was sort of frozen. Not pleasant, not unpleasant, just no feeling at all. He felt dizzy and spaced out in his head. Finally he fell asleep.

His survival system had changed from flee or fight to freezing mode. This is the last stage of defence, when nothing else seems to help, it is also known as the "pretend to be dead reflex".

Those of you who have ever experienced a panic attack or even a phobia know what the little Golden had to endure during this scenario which happens more or less just like that to countless puppies all over the world. You know exactly how it feels when your body takes over your mind and stress hormones run the show.

⊃ Does this sound familiar?

And those of you who have experienced depression know how it feels when you finally give in and get used to conditions which make you feel unhappy and unsafe.

All of us know how terrible it is when your mother leaves you behind as a young child.

Having helped hundreds of people getting over all sorts of panic disorders and phobias as well as having had a phobia myself I am aware of the amount of suffering you have to endure when your sympathetic nervous system starts dominating your parasympathetic nervous system and cortisol and adrenaline flood your body. It seems as though there is nothing you can do about it, and you just have to wait until it's over.

At this point I hear some of you exclaim: "But wait, Martina, that's us, humans, that's not dogs! Surely dogs don't feel the same as we do!" Well, I am afraid they do! Thanks to modern technology scientists were able to find out that our dogs suffer the same way we do. Saliva testing has shown how the cortisol levels rise in his body when the dog is under stress. Dogs are mammals just as we are and they are hard-wired the same way.

Why is it such a big deal for a puppy to be on his own?

Remember that dogs are sociable animals and that in nature pack animals such as dogs are not seen on their own. They are always with others whether hunting, playing, feeding the young or resting. So it is a quite unnatural thing for a dog to be without his family and yet it is something that modern life forces dogs to endure.

You pick a puppy and he comes to your house at an age of seven or eight weeks. WEEKS!

The puppy, if he was left with his mother would be still be drinking milk. The mother would slowly stop feeding him her milk but she would come and bring him food, carrying it in her stomach regurgitating it, so the puppy could eat the pre-digested food. And on no account would the puppy leave the siblings and the den to be on his own. His actual programming is completely different to what we expect of him.

People get puppies and they leave them on their own at the age of 10 weeks. Some even make the young puppy spend his first night alone in the kitchen! This is not only heartless but it also causes separation anxiety. It can either cause separation anxiety or

⊃ Being on their own is not a natural state for social animals

cause depression. Whether you notice it or not, it is not beneficial for your puppy's development to leave him without human company for any length of time when he or she is still a baby.

We can't argue with Nature's laws, we can't persuade her that what worked out well over millennia is now suddenly wrong because we have taken over. If we want our Golden puppies to be happy we need to respect Mother Nature's Laws.

The fully grown and mature Golden Retriever can be left on his own for five hours without suffering. But if you leave him on his own for more than five hours you are really pushing your luck.

This is when your Golden Retriever is mature, when he is self-confident, when he feels safe within himself and safe within his environment, i.e. your home, or when you are traveling in a hotel room or the car.

As a puppy parent, you naturally ask yourself how long can I leave my little puppy alone for and how can I teach him to spend time on his own. Well, the answer is this: You cannot leave a puppy on his own for any amount of time. For a young puppy to be on his own, it means certain death. Other animals can come and eat him. When mother isn't there he is in extreme danger. Since you have taken over mother's role, this means that if you aren't there, or to be more precise, if no human being is around the puppy feels extremely threatened. He just cannot bear being left on his own.

So for the first four to five weeks you should really make it a point of taking your puppy wherever you go. If you go from one room to the other, take her with you. If you have to go outside to put up the washing, take her with you. This is of course a very strenuous thing because it means you really cannot go anywhere. And this is why it is so very important that you have set up a puppy parent support system of friends and family who will take over when you feel that you have had enough of being inside all the time or when you actually need to go out somewhere. I will elaborate on the puppy parent support system a little further down the line.

Teaching puppy to be on his own

When your puppy is twelve weeks old you can try to leave him on his own for a minute or two.

Here is how to set this up:

⮑ Watch your pup's reactions.

▶ Just go outside, leave the room *without* closing the door and then come back in again at once. Notice how your puppy reacts. If she takes no notice and she is quiet and everything is ok, you can then continue with the regime of going outside for a minute or two or three minutes at the most.

▶ Stand outside the door and if you hear her cry you know you have over done it. Next time stay outside for a shorter period of time.

▶ You actually need to come back in before she gets upset. Always work up to that "before" point and you will be able to expand the comfort zone.

▶ With me, I find it most rewarding to let my puppy decide and when the puppy goes into another room on her own and settles down to go to sleep 'far away from me' I know that she is slowly training herself to be without me.

▶ As time goes by you can stretch the minutes. When you leave the puppy, just quietly leave and when you come back, quietly come back in.

- Don't make a fuss when you leave like saying "oh mummy has got to go" and "mummy will be back in a minute and don't you get worried" because that hypes her up. It gets her all excited and she thinks something nice is coming, but what is coming instead is a period of being on her own.

- Take it really slowly, progress in very small steps, not overdoing it.

- Give her something to chew when you leave her for a few minutes give her a big biscuit, something to enjoy whilst you are not with her.

By doing it that way you are training her that it is alright and that you will come back.

What you should not do is give her any treats when you come back because you think "oh, she has been a good girl now I am going to reward her". The reward is your return.

When she comes up to you then greet her as well and be nice and kind with her.

There are those who say that separation anxiety is made worse or even caused by the owner making a fuss of the dog when returning home. This runs under the assumption that the dog is waiting for the master and if the master comes home the dog is very happy and the master is also very happy. This mutual display of happiness is supposed to – in some very strange way – make the dog wait more for the owner and to worsen or create separation anxiety.

This is why old school dog training tells you not to greet your dog when he comes up to greet you when you've been out somewhere. This actually amounts to ignoring your dog when he comes to the door to greet you.

This is a mere assumption! As we have seen, separation anxiety is due to stress hormones flooding the body during the period in which the young animal is kept on his own much against Mother Nature's laws.

Now I personally think ignoring your pup when he wants to lavish you with his love is a kind of emotional abuse.

If you take our three questions: *"Am I loving? Am I consistent? Am I acting wisely?"* you would be asking yourself: is it really loving to ignore my dog when he comes to greet me?

Or if you simply use the two most powerful questions of all: *Would I like to be treated that way and how would I feel if I were my dog?* You'd soon find out that doing it that way is not very kind and to a degree inhumane and perhaps a very much last century approach to dealing with your dog's emotions.

Facts to consider

(only for those that are really interested in details)

The key in training your dog to bear being on his own is training him to feel safe and secure without you being in the same room or in the same house as he is. What are you actually training? His emotions? His behaviour? His psyche?

No, you are actually training his nervous system. Because, as we have seen, the actual problem in separation anxiety is that the autonomic nervous system gets disrupted.

Normally the autonomic nervous system works so that when the parasympathetic nervous system is active, the state is relaxed and calm. One can sleep, think or dream. The whole feeling in the body is that of harmony and peace.

And when the sympathetic nervous system takes and switches off the parasympathetic nervous system the body immediately switches to survival mode.

What you are trying to achieve in taking **baby steps** towards leaving your pup on his own, is actually expanding the time the sympathetic nervous takes before it kicks in.

You do this by expanding that time frame in which your dog still feels comfortable and well, because the parasympathetic nervous system is still active.

The moment the sympathetic nervous system takes over is the moment that the dog becomes nervous, feeling frightened, under stress and starts his stress hormone reducing behaviour. All this is autonomically driven and is not under the control of your dog. Your dog's mind has no say in the matter.

⮑ Be aware that your pup is helpless and relies on you

As you know for yourself, if you have ever experienced a state of panic, the moment the anxiety starts and gets past a certain point there is nothing, absolutely nothing you can do to stop it. The same is actually true for horses. The moment a horse's sympathetic nervous system gets triggered the amygdala is activated, the nervous system changes and the sympathetic nervous system starts running the show. The horse gets into a frenzy and runs and the rider cannot do anything about it. The old brain, the survival system has completely taken over. But it is out of control because the conscious mind and conscious brain are far too slow to guarantee survival. With a dog that suffers from separation anxiety the unpleasant feelings don't subside before the owner is back.

And once the dog has experienced this terrible state, he is now afraid of re-experiencing this state. This is what people who suffer from anxiety disorder teach us. They say "My God, I am so afraid of getting into the panic state again".

The same thing happens with the dog. The dog now fears this very unpleasant state. So he watches his owner closely. What is she doing? Is she putting on her jacket? Is she putting on her coat?
Is she picking up the lead or is she picking up the car keys? Has she got her good shoes on that mean I can't come? Or is she putting on her rubber boots that mean I can come?

The dog is now watching for clues and is getting excited before the owner has actually left. And when the owner has left, panic starts and again there is nothing at all the dog can do about it.

Accordingly the task is to help the dog stay in a relaxed state whilst you are away. As with all tasks for the nervous system you start with little baby steps. So that the time of feeling well, of feeling secure, of being under the influence of the parasympathetic nervous system gets longer and longer and longer.

As you continue training her over weeks to just feel comfortable without you for a longer and longer periods of time and to develop trust that you will return and to also develop the trust that no predator is coming into the house to eat her she will slowly build the strength, trust and endurance she needs to stay on her own.

"Yes", you say, "but I do have to leave my puppy and I do have to go to work and its ok when you just work at home or your take your puppy to the office, but I do have to leave my puppy at the end of three weeks of the vacation I have taken from work to look after her."

We all have that problem!

Use your Puppy Parenting Support System!

Get somebody in to look after your puppy whilst you are out. Or take your puppy to a friend's house or to somewhere like a puppy kindergarten or a puppy nursery where the puppy is not left on his own.

⊃ Rely on your puppy parenting support system.

But if you do have to take your puppy some other place, remember that she needs to get used to the strange surroundings first. Why? Because your puppy is attached to the surroundings of your home. The younger the puppy is the more attached to the surroundings she is rather than being attached to the people who live there because for the young puppy in nature it is the den that means safety.

From a puppy's perspective your kitchen is an enormous universe. And from the puppy's perspective your whole house is vast. Taking the puppy out of that vast universe and placing her in strange vast universe can also be traumatizing for her. So the best bet really is to get somebody in to look after the puppy so that she doesn't have to be alone.

➲ How
about using a
crate then?

Wouldn't a crate serve the same purpose?

Caging dogs in your home is a very fashionable thing to do. It is also one of those things that are very bad for your puppy.

It is bad for his physical development and bad for his emotional development too. The crates were invented by clever people who found a way of making some money. They slowly made their way across the world and they are now almost everywhere. Many, many dogs are being subjected to being kennelled in the house. Some countries have rules and regulations about kennel sizes when dogs are kennelled outside, but most people who get a crate don't think about this.

The crate is usually chosen just large enough for the dog to lie in, to stand up in and maybe to turn around in. There would be no room left in your kitchen if the crate was big enough for the dog's physical needs.

From the physical point of view, this is very sad for the dogs because they need to change places quite frequently. A dog will go to sleep in one position, then get up and go back to sleep somewhere else. This is one of their inborn behaviours which causes *no harm* and *creates no problem* in the average household.

Moving around is necessary for their well being; they can not do this if they are kept in a cage.

Some people think that a Golden Retriever puppy shouldn't move around a lot because of the development of the hips and bones. So they get into the habit of crating their puppy or keeping the puppy confined to a very small space.

⮑ Myth: Golden Retriever puppies should be crated in order to prevent them from moving around a lot.

But the catch is this: puppies need to run, jump, explore and move around. When a puppy is not allowed to move, his muscles and nervous system do not develop properly, and so his intelligence is impaired. When forced to sit there all the time he is deprived of all the sensory input needed to develop neural pathways for canine cleverness and intelligence.

The idea that dogs feel safe when they are in a confined place supported the marketing strategies of crate manufacturers. From there it was only a small step to introducing into dog owner's minds the assumption that it is actually good for the dog to have a place which only belongs to him where nobody else goes.

Being a firm believer of the Truth Principle, that is building my actions and opinions on scientific knowledge rather than myths, I doubt very much that dogs actually have the concept of owning something as a personal belonging. As highly sociable beings they have no idea of the concept "mine or thine".

A dog simply calls nothing his own because he does not know what the concept even means! He will try to get something he likes and sometimes even defend it from other members of his pack. But that is a *moment to moment* decision. That thing will be given up again when the dog's interest in it has faded. This also applies to resting places. An elder or authority figure will claim a certain place to rest on when she feels like it and give it up again when she doesn't feel like it anymore.

When the elder has lost interest in something she is also not interested who has it or uses it.

Having shared my life with up to six Goldens at a time and having been friends with people who keep even more Goldens I was able to watch this happen time after time. Never have I seen a dog act on the principle of "this belongs to me and therefore you can't have it". It's always been "you can't have it *now* because I want it *now*. Whatever happens with it when I don't want it anymore does not bother me at all".

That is quite different from our point of view: We own something and we decide who uses it and when. We feel responsible for it and care for it.

Dogs feel responsible for the members of their family and care for them. They don't care for lifeless objects like we do.

This does not mean that some dogs can not be quite possessive about objects or food and become rather aggressive if either is taken away from them. However this may be, a Golden Retriever was bred so that he would not be possessive over his prey. Otherwise he could not have been used in the field the way he was supposed to be. If a Golden in a human family defends his food or toys something has gone wrong somewhere – either in his genetic makeup or in his socialisation.

When it comes to safety aspect I want my dogs to feel safe anywhere in their home. They don't need a cage or box to feel safe in, because they know that they are absolutely safe where they live.

It never serves the benefit of a dog to be shut away in a small space he can not get out of.
It never serves his development or personality to be shut away from being close to his family members. If crates serve anything it is the convenience of the dog owners.

For hundreds of years you could find dogs under peoples tables and their puppies under their beds. Yes, dogs have an affinity to having a roof over their heads, it reminds them of being in a den. But does this mean they like being shut away from their masters and human family members?
As a new Golden Retriever puppy parent you get to decide on the emotions and feelings of another being, as well as deciding on the shape of his body and overall physiology.

⊃ Dogs should feel safe anywhere in their home

⊃ Crates only serve the convenience of the dog owners

What does life experience as well as science teach us about putting pups into crates?

You might like to consider the following:

➲ Consider this case:

I once worked with a 9 month old female who couldn't be walked along the road by her new owner because she would try to jump at cars.

At car parks she would always try to get into the back of any car and she was nervous and tried to hide wherever the new parents took her. So she couldn't be taken to restaurants as she would get into a frenzy, nor could she be taken to visit the home of friends, let alone be left in a hotel room. All this caused her new owner to ask me for help. The problems cleared within ten most remarkable sessions of EFT, the Emotional Freedom Technique created by Gary Craig. EFT is also known as "Tapping" and is very useful when it comes to solving emotional and stress related problems in people and animals alike.

➲ Emotional Freedom Technique or "Tapping".

During the treatment it became evident that young Bessie had been subjected to long and lonely hours of being shut away in a crate. The other dogs of her family were allowed to play but Bessie was kept in the crate and only allowed out for short periods of playing ball with one of the sons. Those countless hours inside the box had severely traumatized her and had kept her away from learning that the world was a safe place. Thus she was afraid whenever she was outside her crate. Hence she wanted to get into cars because she had found out that they are crates of a sort too.

Interesting, isn't it?

The other unpleasant side effect of crating a puppy is that when in a crate he can not follow you around and yes, many people put their puppies in crates so they don't follow them around.

But those are the same people who *later* in their dog's life complain that he takes off on his own in the forest or in the field and chases other animals and doesn't come back when called.

This has to do with the early frustration of the inborn need to follow.

As said before the young dog is blessed with a system of automatic behaviours which secures survival. One of these automatic behaviour instincts is the drive to follow mother wherever she goes.

⊃ Crates prevent your pup from following you...

⊃ ... possibly resulting in taking off, chasing animals and not coming back when called.

⊃ Puppies have an inborn need to follow.

There is no animal in the wild who has its baby on a lead to make sure the baby doesn't run away. No cat mother has her kittens on a lead. And no canine mother has her puppies on a lead. This is because mothers know intuitively that their puppies will actually follow her around wherever she goes and this is what puppies actually do.

Mothers lead, and puppies follow.

The puppy needs to need you. As long as a dog needs his people he will stay with them.

⮑ The puppy needs to need you.

The worst thing that can happen to any Golden Retriever owner is for his dog to feel independent and to be in "I please myself" mode. That is when the dog does whatever the dog wants to do. So that when you let him off the lead he goes off and off he is – because he feels safe without you. Since he feels safe and happy without you he can now please himself. That is not at all a good place to be in for you as the owner.

⮑ A pitfall to consider

The first step to this independent behaviour is to actually train your dog to feel independent and to feel well without you by preventing him from attaching himself to you by following you around.

The puppy needs to follow you. This is one of Nature's unbreakable laws. Ignore it and you will have to pay a price.

When you don't allow this by locking him up in a kennel, he will become depressed, become helpless and get into a behaviour called learned depression where he just accepts that he has to be in there. The first days he will fight against it, he will fight, cry, call for mummy and try to get out and get very annoyed.

He is now under the influence of the sympathetic nervous system again because there is this drive called "I need to follow her" but at the same time he realizes that he can't.

⊃ How your puppy feels when crated

Here is what that may well feel like for your puppy:

"I can't. I just can't get out. No matter what I do, no matter how loud I call her, no matter how hard I fight *I can not do anything.*

So what can I do? My drive is putting me under great tension and as with all drives, it grows over time. Lucky for me Nature has provided me with a coping strategy which says: Before an unfulfilled drive kills you the drive will give way and lessen as time goes by. I am still under stress but the stress gets less and less because I need to follow you around less and less. At first I was in fight or flight mode, then I got into the freezing state, now Nature has had mercy on me and my drive to be with you loosens its grip.

Yes, I am happy to get out of my confinement but I have learned to accept that that is just the way my life is. But you know, I can get by and I will. I now know that I can feel okay when I am not with you over long periods of time, that I can hear your voice but that it means nothing to me and so, yes, I am okay.

I even feel quite safe in my box and when the world outside it gets too dangerous I run for it and hide in it. Keeps me safe, you know. Because the world is such a dangerous place to be!"

Whilst this may sound like emotional poetry, take a look at the facts:

Remember that when it is endangered the animal can fight, flee or freeze. The freezing behaviour is very quiet, doesn't move and actually appears to be very calm and collected or dead. When a young puppy is put in a crate, the crate door is closed, he naturally fights to get out and after a while gives up the fighting, crying and barking. The owners then think he is now used to being in there and has happily accepted being in the crate. It's good for him and we are doing the right thing.

The contrary is true, the puppy gives up, he becomes frustrated, and over time this frustration turns into a state of learned helplessness and so he seems to accept the adverse conditions.

But accepting adverse conditions does not mean that they are not going to harm the development of his personality, his emotions and his attachment and bonding with you.

We don't always see the things we cause at the moment we are causing them, do we? This is especially true when it comes to developing beings like a baby or a puppy.

The idea of kennelling a dog is also justified with saying "Well if I kennel him, if I put him in his crate, he will not destroy the furniture and he will not do this and will not do that".

That's just an excuse because he also won't do any of the kind if you train him properly. When you take the time to educate your puppy on things he may chew and not chew and if you take the time of puppy proofing your home, apartment or house then you don't need to crate your puppy.

You don't have to create this massive inner pain in your puppy.

Having discussed some really deep and basic issues let's now get down to the more practical way of doing important things. Again, let's do some Q and A!

Bonding - The Essence Of Love

The quality of the bond between you and your Golden Retriever is of prime importance. Everything that happens in your dog 's life is mediated by your mutual bond and because of this you need to take special care when it comes to bonding with your puppy.

Q: What does the term Bonding actually mean?

A: Bonding refers to building a relationship, establishing a close connection, the building of a bond. It is a psychological term used to describe the way individuals get close to each other. Psychologists investigating child development have found out that the bond between a baby and her primary caretakers sets the stage for her emotional, physical, mental as well as her social development.

Q: And what has all this got to do with me and my Golden Retriever puppy?

A: Almost every animal on the planet is hard wired to bond with other members of his species. The bond which is formed very early in life makes sure that the young animal feels safe and secure. This feeling of safety enables the youngster to explore the world around him, to learn and to develop a healthy sense of self. Without the creation of a bond between members of a family no social setting may exist.

An animal can only be a member of a pack or herd or any kind of group if such a bond exists. It is the bond which "glues" individuals to each other and without it members of a group would attack and hurt each other or the group would just drift apart. No group or couple can exist without the process of bonding

This means that the moment your Golden Retriever puppy has the opportunity to bond with anyone she will do so. Your puppy needs to form a bond with some other being and she will do so.

Establishing a bond takes time and physical closeness.

If you want your puppy to bond with you, you need to spend time in close contact with him.

Here is how you set this up:

Sit on the floor with him as often a possible, let him sleep on your lap, let him sit by your feet. Allow your puppy to follow you around. Puppies are born followers, it is one of their basic instincts, is to follow their mother wherever she goes. Think of yourself as your pup's mummy and let him be with you as much as he wants to be.

Indeed the bond you form with your pup replaces the bond he did already have with his mother before he was taken away from her.

Q: Is that all there is to it? Cuddling her, spending time, playing little games? Is it really that easy?

A: Yes, it is the most natural thing in the world and all natural things come easy. As long as you do not stop or hinder your Golden Retriever puppy she will form a very strong bond with you.

Q: Hinder her? How would I do that when I want our bond to be strong?

A: By stopping her natural behaviour.

       This is why putting puppies in a crate is such a very bad idea.
       Because:
       ▶ Your puppy needs to be with you,
       ▶ to feel you
       ▶ and to smell you – not to look at you through the bars of some indoor kennel

If you rob your pup of the chance to be with you whenever she needs to you will impair the bonding behaviour which is most active in a very young canine. Most behaviour problems in Golden Retrievers have their origin in some early bonding problem.

The bond between you and your adult Golden Retriever strongly depends on the quality of the early bonding. This is why you need to take extra care during your puppy's first month with you

Here is the tip:

Make sure to take a vacation when you get your puppy. Make sure your puppy is not left alone in the first two or three months of her life with you. Ask family members to stay with him or her when you need to go out.

Remember: A Golden Retriever wants to be with his significant other as much as possible. He is **not** made to be on his own for countless hours.

Your Golden Retriever puppy needs your time and presence to securely bond with you, and to grow into the Golden Retriever of your dreams!

Tips For Your Puppy's First Nights With You

⊃ Your puppy can't be happy on his first night without you.

Today is the great day you have been waiting for! You are finally bringing your Golden Retriever puppy home! You have been waiting for this moment to arrive for quite a while, anticipating a life full of joy and happiness together with your new friend.

If you have a family your kids and spouse are just as excited as your are. The excitement grows as you park your car in front of your breeder's house, eager to welcome the brand new family member.

The puppies are now around seven to eight weeks old. They have been with their mother and siblings for most of their short lives. Their entire life time was spend with their breeder, either in their kennel or, if you have chosen a very dedicated breeder, in his house and garden.

Whether your Golden Retriever puppy was asleep or awake, he was always in the company of other canines, experiencing the warmth of their bodies, their odours and the security such close canine companionship afforded them.

But now you have come to take your puppy away with you, away from his siblings and his mother, away from the breeder who looked after him.

Your Golden Retriever puppy is seven to eight weeks old. He does not know anything about you and your family. He has no idea that in a few moments time he will be in a completely different world from the one he knew.

Imagine, how that little puppy is going to feel for the next few days until he has gotten used to his new environment.

The first and most dominant feeling will be that of fear and loneliness. There will be so many new things to cope with, all the new and bewildering smells and stimuli. But most of all, his mummy and siblings will not be there, no matter how much he will be calling them.

Now comes his first night in your home. His first night without the warmth and comfort of sleeping close to another dog.

This is going to be a very difficult experience for your puppy, no matter how you organize it.

It is you who decides whether his first night in your house is going to be a traumatic experience or just a difficult one.

How can you make sure to keep his suffering as small as possible?

▶ Allow your Golden Retriever puppy to spend the night with you!

▶ Allow him to come and cuddle up to you if he wants to, to feel the warmth and reassuring presence of your body.

This way you not only spare him a lot of heartache, you also speed up the bonding process between the pair of you.

I know that the standard piece of advice is to put a Golden Retriever puppy in a crate on his first night, or to leave him in his box in the kitchen.

This is very cruel advice without consideration for the emotional well-being of the baby.

Here is the tip:

Your best bet would be to make yourself a comfortable bed on the floor in your bedroom or the living room so your puppy has access to you during the night. I have had many puppies over the years and this worked exceptionally well. The puppy got used to me in no time, there was hardly any crying at night.

After a few weeks my pups are usually able to sleep without "Mummy" and I return to my bed in the bedroom.

If you can not convince yourself to share your night with your puppy on the floor, your second best way to do it is this:

Find a cardboard box big enough to allow your puppy ample room to lie down in and make a comfortable bed for her by putting in a soft cushion. Make sure the box is too high for your pet to climb out of and place the box next to your bed. If and when your Golden puppy cries at night, you can pet him and soothe his distress. If he needs to do his business he will wake you up so you can take him outside.

This arrangement allows you the comfort of your bed without leaving your little one in despair.

Here is the important message:

Because it is your goal to raise an emotionally sound Golden Retriever you need to take extra care to minimize the amount of distress your animal needs to endure.

For this you will be rewarded time and time again with a dog who is securely bonded to you, who is calm and collected and does not have separation anxiety or other emotional problems.

It is really easy! All you need to do is listen to your heart and treat your puppy as the fragile little being he really is.

The amount of empathy, time, patience and effort you invest into his development will bless you with the canine companion of your dreams.

Teaching And Educating Your Puppy

*Bonding with your puppy may begin
whilst he is still with his breeder*

⊃ Let's try to put ourselves into our pup's place...

How puppies learn

From a puppy's mouth

Just like all living beings out there I have but one principle:

I want to feel well and I want to avoid feeling unwell.

▶ I learn to do the things that give me a good feeling.
▶ I don't do things that make me feel bad.
▶ When I do something and it does not give me good feelings I will just give up doing it.
▶ If it gave me good feelings initially and does not give me good feelings anymore I will forget about it.

▶ Because I depend on the fact that nothing bad happens to me I am always a little alert and ready to shy away from it

▶ If something really gave me a bad time, I will try to avoid it in the future. If this is not possible I run away or I will attack. And when that isn't possible I will pretend to be dead and hope for the best.

My feelings and behaviours are run by my brain.

My brain sends its messages to my body via neurotransmitters but also via electrical impulses directly to the nerve cells. The messages go through the nerve cells into my body, organs and systems. I have a central nervous system as well as an autonomic nervous system. The latter is very important in regards to my feelings because when the parasympathetic nervous system is active I feel well, happy and satisfied.

When my sympathetic nervous system gets activated I get upset, feel fear, have pain or sense a danger. Being nervous is always a sign that my sympathetic nervous system is activated.

▶ Learning is easiest for me when I am relaxed, not nervous, not in pain or frightened. I can't learn when I am in pain.

▶ This means in order to learn something I have to feel safe and secure.

▶ The only thing I learn when I am stressed, upset, feeling unsafe and insecure, is learning fear and avoidance.

What does it actually mean for me to learn something? It means that certain nerve cells my brain and body start to get into contact with one another to share information and create the habit of doing so more and more often. Over time they create a neural pathway.

There is a principle in neuroscience: "Neurons that fire together wire together". This is known to you people as 'Hebb's Law'.

Via the synapses the nerve cells in my brain and body exchange information and they actually get used to working together. By doing this, my brain builds new neural networks and when that has happened I am able to do something new, respectively, that a certain behaviour becomes a habit of mine.

Let me give you an example of how this works for me:

When you first called me for dinner I didn't know what you meant...

Then I noticed that I would get something to eat if I ran towards you at the sound of that word...

This was just because it felt right for me to run to you at the time...

There was no purpose in it...

➲ Here is a real-life example on how I learn.

But then I realized that the word "Dinner" means something great. Over time the neurons, the nerve cells in my body, responsible for running towards you at the sound of that word started to fire together. So when I hear that word now I just run towards you whenever and wherever.

I can not do anything about it, it just happens.

My brain and body have made it a new habit. I always do it now because it gives me such a good feeling.

But: I will soon forget about it again if it does not make me happy anymore! So your best bet is to always make me happy when I come to you!

In order for me to learn something new I need to repeat and practice doing it over quite a long time. Because my neurons need time to get used to talking with each other and to connect to each other reliably.

If you want me to learn something completely new, my brain must create new neuronal pathways. That which I am to learn has to settle in.

▶ Therefore it is best if you teach me one thing at a time and make sure I don't get too distracted.

▶ And it also would be good if you gave me a little rest after our short lessons.

▶ By the way, I can not concentrate for long, so our lessons must be short. Five minutes at the most!

▶ Better to teach me a lesson twice a day for five minutes than to "work" with me ten minutes at a time.

I just can't cope with that. After we have been working on a new learning task, let's just sit quietly for a few minutes so my brain can work out what it all means and how to do it in future.

I know that you people are a little impatient. So I'd better tell you right away that it can take up to **three weeks** for me to learn something.

You will know that my brain has completed the neural pathway creation when I *always, that is each and every time, do the new thing you ask me to do.*

If I only do it now and then it has not yet become my automatic response to your words because the necessary neural pathways in my nervous system have not been completed. Therefore I still have to think about it and I still have a choice. When the process has been completed I don't have that choice anymore. I simply must do what you say because that's how my brain has been wired.

⮑ Otherwise you'll have to repeat it... I'm sorry for this, but that's how my brain works

I know that this may sound a bit complicated to you and perhaps you have never thought about my learning like this but this how it is!

What You Need To Know About
Teaching Your Puppy

When you think about training your dog, you have two possible scenarios:

1. The dog is supposed to learn a desired behaviour.
2. He has created some bad habits you want him to unlearn, i.e. not to perform the unwanted behaviour any more.

For the development of behavioural patterns and problem solving Mother Nature has also created some very powerful, universal laws. The Laws Of Learning.

Here they are:

➲ The Laws of Learning

The **first** one is that a behaviour which leads to a pleasant inner state will probably be used more often in the future.

The **second** law is that a behaviour which leads to an unpleasant inner state will probably be used less often in future.

The **third** law is that a behaviour which does not lead to any kind of inner change will be be used less and less until it is not used anymore at all.

The **additional** law is that reward is much more effective than punishment.

▶ In order for something to be learned, the reward has to follow the behaviour *immediately*.

▶ In order for a behaviour to be eliminated, the punishment has to follow *immediately*.

It is essential that the reaction follows ***immediately*** after the action because then and only then can the nerve cells in the brain make a connection between the action and it's consequence. If there is a time lapse, the connection will not be made because it is always the last shown behaviour right before the reaction which is either rewarded or punished.

In order for the brain to connect two stimuli these have to appear simultaneously or at least almost simultaneously.

Example:

You and your pooch are in the park together. You call him and he doesn't come. You call him five times and after the sixth time you've called him he finally comes and you tell him off. You think that you have told him off for running away and for not coming when he was called.

In truth you are actually punishing him for coming to you because it is always the behaviour shown just before the punishment or the reward which gets connected to the response. Do this two or three times and your dog will avoid coming to you even more. And rightfully so!

When your little puppy jumps on the sofa, pulls down one of your cushions and brings it to you and you scold him for having taken the cushion, you will actually teach him over time not to retrieve. Because he cannot connect what he brought to you with your reaction but he connects the fact that he brought something to you with your punishment.

It is of utmost importance to remember that it is

▶ always the behaviour shown immediately **before** the reward which is being reinforced.

▶ always the behaviour shown immediately **before** the punishment that is being punished.

This point can not be overstressed because it is of vital importance when it comes to training anyone, be it puppy, child, student or yourself.

If you take this single message from the entire book and make it your own you will be well on the way to being the perfect teacher for anyone!

One big mistake people make is that they go to great length to teach their puppy something new and when the puppy has learnt it and does it they forget to reward him for doing it.

This causes the behaviour to be deleted in the long run because it is of no use anymore in the sense that the puppy doesn't gain any pleasure through doing it.

▶ So please do make sure to always praise your puppy for being obedient and doing what you have asked her to do!

Here is the Golden Rule

▶ Make sure you always recognize the things your dog does for you by at least giving him a pat or a kind word.

▶ Make sure that being obedient always makes him feel good and reward him with some attention

Most Important!

If your dog has started teaching himself a kind of behaviour which you don't really want him to do or you have started teaching the unwanted behaviour yourself and you want to end it bear this in mind:

It is very important that you must never ever reward this behaviour again because if the behaviour brings success only once in a while it is strengthened – even if this success only happens once in two months.

The behaviour is strengthened by the so-called intermittent reward. This works for desirable and undesirable behaviour alike.

It is one of the "sad" facts of dog training that we often teach our dogs undesirables behaviour by handing out rewards carelessly or in the wrong context.

Remember This:

Your puppy is learning all the time. Her 'brain is out for gain'. She is watching out for clues, trying to make sense of each and everything you do. She is interested in feeling good. Feeling good is caused by food, so she is always looking out for something to eat and chew. She can learn to connect praise with food and so your praise can become a reward in itself over time.

You have to be very careful not to teach her something undesirable by accident. Therefore you need to watch yourself and your family members and anyone who comes into contact with her.

Emotions are also learned and your puppy may learn to fear certain things because they caused her bad feelings or pain. These things can happen accidently as well.

You need to know what you want in order to get it, right?

When it comes to teaching and educating your puppy it is of utmost importance to be really clear on your goals to make sure your actions get you and your puppy in the right directions.

Teaching puppies undesirable behaviours is very easy and happens very fast. It is only when you watch and monitor yourself closely and by structuring her environment so that nothing can go wrong will you be able to avoid teaching her the worst ones.

Nobody is perfect and we all make our mistakes with our puppies but we can and must do our best to set things up so that she can be happy and healthy during her lifetime with us.

9 Steps and Principles for creating a wonderful life

Happy again at last

#1 **Set Up A Puppy Parenting Support System**

Looking after your puppy is going to keep you occupied for quite a number of weeks. In order to avoid over-stressing yourself you should set up a support system of people who will help you take care of your youngster. This may be family and friends but also 13 to 16 year old girls or boys from the neighbourhood who are always happy to help out for some small rewards. Make sure you have plenty of people who are willing and able to help out so that you don't feel locked in with your puppy.

#2 **Puppy Proof Your House and Home!**

Puppies are inquisitive and love to investigate and explore their world. They have sharp little teeth. They do not come when called and they do not do as they are told. Puppies love licking – living and non living objects. Puppies love chewing – Puppies love pulling on things – Puppies love taking things apart.

In short: Puppies can be a right menace at times.

This is why you need to prepare your home for the arrival of your sweet little Golden Retriever puppy!

When it comes to preparing the house your first aim is to create a safe environment for the new baby. Make sure that the youngster can not get at any:

- ▶ wires
- ▶ technical or electrical instruments
- ▶ hoses
- ▶ curtainsloose fittings
- ▶ papers or magazines
- ▶ documents
- ▶ pens and writing equipment
- ▶ children's toys

You need to put away any expensive or otherwise valuable carpets, rugs or blankets in order to protect them from sharp Golden Retriever puppy teeth.

Don't forget your table and chair legs since they make wonderful gnawing opportunities. One way to protect them would be to wrap some bandages around them so they can not be scratched.

Put away all vases and flower pots which you keep on the floor – a Golden Retriever puppy running around is very likely to break things without meaning to.

Make sure he can not get at any of your house plants or plants which are poisonous.

Should you or a member of your family smoke make very sure that puppy can not get at the cigarettes.

Eating just one cigarette will kill him.
The same goes for chocolates. Chocolate poisoning is very dangerous for a dog.

It is a good idea to get some form of children's door gates so you can block off certain rooms and the stairs.

If you have small kids you need to make sure your puppy can not get into their rooms and they don't leave their toys around for a while because puppies swallow things that can may make them seriously ill.

Make sure your garden is Golden Retriever puppy safe by fencing off any poisonous plants.

If your garden has access to a street or road make sure the puppy can't get out. This may mean making the fences stronger at the bottom so your puppy will not be successful at digging his way out.

You may think "oh, why make such a fuss of all this – it will be alright on the day", but let me assure you that a healthy lively puppy is full of mischief and will turn your place upside down in no time!

By preparing your house and making it puppy safe you avoid danger, minimize stress and maximize happiness and pleasure for all of you.

By preparing your house and making it puppy safe you avoid danger, minimize stress and maximize happiness and pleasure for all of you. Creating safety both for your puppy and your furniture is fairly easy if you take a close look around.

The changes you make now can be undone when your puppy is a bit older and has gone through his teething stages.

#3 **Get very clear on your goals** and ask your family and friends whether you are sending out unclear or mixed messages

#4 **Monitor your own behaviour** towards your puppy. Be really honest with yourself and ask family members to tell you if you are really being consistent and clear.

#5 **Discuss the issue of puppy education** with your partner (if you live in a close relationship) and make sure both of you use the same commands and implement the same rules.

#6 **Make sure to educate your kids** and everyone who has access to your puppy on your goals and on how you would like your puppy to be treated.

#7 **Don't be a perfectionist!** Everyone makes mistakes and there is a learning curve for each and every one of us.

#8 **Don't lose your humour**, try to see the funny side of things. After all, that carpet can be cleaned and that mess can be cleaned up.

#9 **Always listen to your heart.** Your deep inner feelings allow you to connect with your puppy at a soul level. Let your heart guide you and show your affection freely.

Take wise and loving action right away!

Take Action Now!

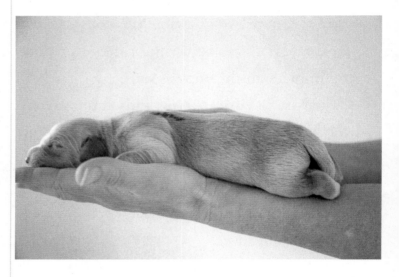

My life and happiness are in your hands

Your First Step

Now, right after you have finished reading, I would like you to go through your house or flat, inspect your garden to see if there is anything your puppy could destroy which you would not like to be destroyed.

Remember:

▶ If puppy can get it he will.
▶ If puppy can chew it she will.
▶ If it is breakable, it will get broken.

Make sure nothing of any importance can be damaged by your puppy. Remove those carpets.

Find a way of protecting your curtains. Do what ever it takes so that you can really relax and just enjoy being with your puppy instead of worrying about the safety of your home.

Your Second Step

When you have done that, take your puppy into your arms and stand together with her in front of a large mirror.

Look at the pair of you in the mirror and promise her and yourself that you will always do your best to get present day knowledge about her training and healthcare so that she will always be safe with you.

Tell her how happy you are because she is now part of your life and thank her for being there with you. Feel the love flowing from your heart to her heart and feel her love for you.

And then promise yourself to value and enjoy each and every day with your wonderful little puppy.

Take a vow to be happy with her, because love and happiness are the reasons and the rewards for sharing your life with a Golden Retriever.

Dear Golden Lover,

thank you for reading this book and taking to heart the secrets of raising a Golden Puppy who listens and loves you back.

I hope you enjoyed our journey together as much as I enjoyed writing it.

At the time of writing this (2017) I have shared my life with our wonderful breed for 42 years and I can honestly say that my dogs have rewarded me for everything I have done for them.

When you first get a puppy it is all roses but as times goes by there will be the odd thorn and there will be pain and heartache along the way.

But I can assure you, the love of your Golden will make up for everything.

It is my sincere wish for you and your baby that you become the great team you are meant to be. That your mutual love and understanding grows over time as your friendship deepens.

Please let me know how you are getting on and if you found my book to be helpful. I'd love to hear your story and see a pic of you and your little one who will soon grow into a big and strong Golden.

If you have any questions or problems, just send me an email : martinabecher@web.de

Join our facebook group : Golden Puppy Book https://www.facebook.com/groups/GoldenPuppyBook where you can share your stories with others who also own the book and are on the same journey to more love and understanding and deeper connection with their Goldens.

This group is the best place for sharing and connecting - but you will also find more tips and secrets to create the one in a lifetime relationship with your Golden Retriever.

See you there!

With Love

Martina

Made in the USA
Monee, IL
18 May 2022

96615006R00121